D0946413

REAL ESTATE
GAMEChangers™

Published by CelebrityPress®, Orlando, FL.

CelebrityPress® is a registered trademark.

Printed in the United States of America.

ISBN: 978-0-9983690-3-7
LCCN: 2017932831

For more information, please write:
CelebrityPress®
520 N. Orlando Ave, #2
Winter Park, FL 32789
or call 1.877.261.4930

Visit us online at: www.CelebrityPressPublishing.com

REAL ESTATE GAMEChangers™

CelebrityPress®
Winter Park, Florida

CONTENTS

CHAPTER 1

THE POWER IN THE RIGHT PRICE

BY MICHAEL REESE

Your home is an investment and it should be treated that way. When it comes time to getting a return on that investment when you sell, pricing your home can perhaps be one of the most important tasks in that process.

Price it too high and your home sits on the market – losing you equity with each day that it goes unsold. Price it too low and you're leaving the proverbial money on the table. Most importantly though, the price of your home will help you create a home preparation budget and plan – to ensure that you get the most amount of money when it does sell.

The question is, how do you make sure you do the right things in the right order to price your home well enough, so you can walk away with the most amount of money for your home?

The answer is not as complicated as you might think.

One of the myths in the real estate industry is that homes sell for a fixed price. The truth is that homes actually sell in a range. Some of them sell at the top of the range and others sell at the bottom, which is even the case for homes that appear to be very similar on paper.

After spending more than a decade selling real estate and advising thousands of homeowners on what to do to get top dollar for their home, I've actually experienced the benefits of proactively managing the selling process so that homeowners were able to sell their home at the top of the range.

In fact, I've witnessed the exact same home, in the exact same area, selling for as much as 18% more than the other. The crazy thing is they both sold for list price.

There are logical reasons why some homes sell at the top of the market and others at the bottom. In this scenario, the reason the second home sold for less was because of the owners' motivation and reason: they simply priced the home low to get it sold.

The unfortunate part here was that the sellers' equity in the property was simply transferred to the new homeowner because after the home was appraised, it was worth 'way more' than what it sold for.

This should not surprise anyone; it happens every day. You see people buy homes, fix them up and sell them for more than they originally purchased them. In real estate, we refer to that process as flipping a home and it's something done regularly by real estate investors.

When investors buy homes, they determine what their budget is for fixing the home based on one variable: what the home will sell for once it's fixed. That simple equation determines if the home is a good investment or a bad investment and good investors know that all their decisions hinge on the price of the home.

THREE KEYS TO GETTING THE BEST PRICE

Like an investor, you need to make important decisions about the price of your home, which should ultimately come at the advice of an agent. Essentially, you need to be proactive in managing the process of selling of your home and have a home preparation and budget plan before you list. And, like any good real estate investor, you should make an educated decision on what you're going to do and how much you're going to spend to prepare your home for sale. That all starts by determining two things:

1) What your home would sell for if it were in optimal condition.

2) What needs to be done to get it into that condition.

From my experience, there are three vital things a seller must do in order to ensure they get the most for their home: have the home staged prior to putting it on the market, get a prelisting appraisal and conduct a pre-listing inspection prior to putting it on the market. The successful completion of these three activities virtually ensures that the home will not only be in optimal condition, but also that it will garner a price at the top of its selling range.

As well, there is one intangible benefit to proactively managing the sales process that is sometimes worth more than money, and that's peace of mind. Knowing what issues you're going to face ahead of time and being able to resolve them before they become a problem for the buyer can potentially save you a significant number of headaches along the way.

I. Staging the Home

Now, one of the critical points in the preparation process is to have your home staged by a professional home stager. By proactively managing this part of the process, you make your home shine in the eyes of the buyer because it's clean, well maintained and it looks sharp. Not only does it impact the price the buyer is willing to pay, it can also influence the appraisal price given on the home. A properly staged home can earn up to as much as 6% more than one that is just listed without being staged at all.

Knowing this, you'll want to have the home staged prior to the appraisal and before any marketing or collateral material is created. And, with almost 90% of home buyers starting their home search online, your first showings will likely start on the Internet. Having your home staged ahead of time ensures that the photos of your home are spectacular and give the buyer an excellent first look at what you have to offer.

Unfortunately, simply relying on negotiations to get top dollar is a reactive process that will likely net you less. By staging the home and putting it in optimal condition prior to sale, it will bring a higher price at listing time. From my experience, it takes way less negotiating skills to negotiate a high offer to top dollar than a low offer.

II. Pre-listing Appraisal

Most people know what an appraisal is because it was required by the lender to help protect their investment. Most appraisals are not ordered for the homeowners' benefit, they are ordered for the banks that are lending the money. It's their way of protecting their investment.

An appraisal by textbook definition is an "opinion of value." There are many techniques and choices appraisers have available at their disposal to support their opinion with facts. An appraiser has to have tangible proof in the form of comparable sales that meet Fannie Mae criteria for the purposes of comparison.

There is no required training on how to price a home for real estate agents. Most agents learn to do a CMA to help sellers come up with a price of their home, but the process is so varied and inconsistent across the board that it's not the most reliable means of determining price. This is proven by the fact that the bank uses an appraisal, and not a CMA, as a means of confirming the sales price for the loan.

In my experience, I've never met a homeowner who wanted to reduce the price of their home. I have, however, met many homeowners who have received terrible advice from agents that caused them to get less for their homes. Having a pre-listing appraisal is one way of treating the home as an investment and targeting the best price for your home. Plus, it requires a marginal investment on your part that helps you maximize the value of your home.

III. Pre-listing Inspection

A home inspection is a standard part of the home-buying process and unfortunately, it is the number one reason that a home sale falls apart. In addition to that, the home inspection is the part of the sales process where buyers and the agents who represent them seek to get further price reductions and additional concessions from the seller. It's also one of the greatest causes of headaches and stress for the homeowner.

To prevent all of these things from happening, I've had my sellers conduct a pre-listing inspection on their home. By doing this, the sellers have an opportunity to see what the buyer is going to see before the home goes on the market. As such, they have the ability to resolve any issues that the buyer might use against them in the negotiations.

Additionally, the seller saves a significant amount of money on any repairs that need to be done. Statistically speaking, the expense of having something repaired or replaced once the buyer discovers it during a home inspection can be as much as seven times what the seller would incur to resolve the issue. Most importantly, though, once the issues are resolved, the home is much closer to being in the best shape it can be to attract a higher offer and appraisal price.

What's even better is that the seller now has the inspection results – and proof of any repairs – to provide to prospective buyers to let them know that all the issues have been taken care of. This gives the buyer more peace of mind, confidence about the quality of the home and a better appreciation of why the home is priced as it is. It also prevents the buyer from using the home inspection as a second negotiation on the price of the home.

At this point you might be asking yourself: "Is that all I have to do to get top dollar?" The answer, of course, is a "No." There are over 115 variables that must be proactively managed to help a seller navigate the home-selling process successfully.

That said, these three strategies – home staging, a pre-listing appraisal and a pre-listing inspection – are key elements in making sure that any home listed can justify selling for a price at the top of its range. The investment of time and money on your part is minimal, but the return you receive can mean thousands of dollars in your pocket when you receive top dollar for your home.

About Michael and Jay

More than ten years ago, Jay Kinder and Michael Reese inadvertently caught up with each other one summer afternoon at Lake Texoma. Real estate was the discussion of the day as a young Jay Kinder shared how he sold 233 homes the previous year to a very open-minded Michael Reese. Who knew that a chance encounter would turn into the wildly successful partnership that is now Kinder Reese Real Estate Advisors?

Since that day, Michael, Jay and their teams have sold more than 4,250 homes combined. Together, they've brought in more than $18,000,000 in commissions for their real estate businesses, and haven't looked back since that fateful day.

Both Jay and Michael have been members of *Realtor Magazine*'s prestigious "30 under 30" group. They have also both been ranked within the Top 100 of the 400 most successful real estate teams in North America by Real Trends of *The Wall Street Journal*.

Individually, Jay has established himself as one of the top agents in the world, selling more than 3,000 homes while capturing 14% market share in Lawton, Oklahoma. In 2007, Jay was named #2 in the World for Coldwell Banker, competing with over 120,000 realtors – being the youngest to ever obtain this achievement. The results don't stop there. In 2007, Jay was also ranked #1 in Oklahoma and #2 in the Southern Region including over 1,700 realtors from 14 states. He has been recognized with the honor of #1 Sales Associate in Oklahoma in 2002-2010 before opening his new company, Jay Kinder Real Estate Experts in 2011.

Michael has also enjoyed immense success as one of Keller Williams' top 50 agents worldwide. He is regularly ranked as one of the Top 5 teams in the Southwest Region for Keller Williams, and he and his team recently broke the record for buyer sales for the Keller Williams he worked out of in Frisco, Texas – before going independent as the Michael Reese Home Selling Team. Michael earned $1,000,000 in GCI after only his sixth year in the business and he's never made less since then.

In 2004, Jay and Michael started Kinder Reese Real Estate Partners with the aim of helping success-minded agents like themselves create the business and lifestyle that virtually every real estate agent dreams about. Kinder Reese currently serves more than 23,000 agents across North America with its revolutionary business model and innovative business systems.

In 2011, they co-founded the National Association of Expert Advisors® (NAEA), which offers the most prestigious designations that a real estate agent in today's market can have. The Certified Home Selling Advisor® designee has been recognized as an agent with a highly differentiated, proven, repeatable system to get sellers up to 18% more than the methods of average real estate agents. The NAEA's goal is to provide the highest level of education, training and business materials to agents who are truly serious about bringing the absolute best consumer experience to today's home sellers and buyers.

The Certified Home Selling Advisor® designation is a four-part certification process that helps today's real estate agents learn what they need to truly distinguish themselves from their competition and establish themselves as the true, number one choice for real estate consumers in their marketplace.

They are both best-selling authors on Amazon's Top Ten list of books for small businesses with their book *Trendsetters*, and they can be seen on NBC, ABC, CBS, CNBC and other major networks as Expert Advisors™ on the television show, *The New Masters of Real Estate.*

Currently, Jay lives in Frisco, Texas with his wife, Amber, and has three sons, Brayden, Karsen and Riggs. Michael lives in Frisco, Texas with his wife Stacey and their two sons, Cache and Crew.

CHAPTER 2

HOW TO TURN TOP DOLLAR INTO NET PROFIT — THE SINGLE PAGE THAT WILL DETERMINE HOW MUCH EQUITY YOU WILL WALK AWAY WITH WHEN YOU SELL YOUR HOME

BY JAY KINDER
NAEA CO-FOUNDER

Obviously, this book is focused on selling your home for top dollar. Why would you want to sell for top dollar? Because homes that sell at the top of the market usually sell faster and have less hassles throughout the closing process. "Why?" you ask. Because a home that has been prepared, priced and positioned correctly in the market will give the impression that it is a "good deal" when compared to the rest of the homes in the market. This means you have the opportunity to hit the trifecta, the hat trick, or the turkey – if you are a bowler, when it comes to selling your home and putting the most equity in your pocket at closing.

Tell me if this is accurate. After your home is sold, you want to look back and acknowledge that these three statements are true.

1. My home sold for the most amount of money.
2. My home sold in the time frame I wanted it to sell.
3. The process was smooth and there were no surprises along the way.

You would probably agree that looking back on your home sale, if you can affirm those three things, you would be pretty happy with the real estate agent that helped facilitate the sale of your home, right? Me too.

The number one frustration many homeowners have, but don't think about, is related to the third statement. We are going to remove this threat by understanding the most frustrating part of the home-selling process that could be financially devastating.

Net profit!

At the end of the day, this is the number you care about. "How much money do I walk away with after everything is said and done?" So how do you figure this number out? "Won't every agent prepare me a net sheet related to the home sale so I can see what all the costs related to the sale are?" you ask. Well yes and no.

Yes, actually, it is required by law in most states for the seller to receive an estimate of net proceeds prior to putting the home on the market, and with every written offer you receive.

For your convenience, I've shared a sample document at: www.kinderreese.com/sellernetsheet for you to download and review. I've also included a video walking you through each of the areas I'm about to discuss here so you can accurately determine your net proceeds yourself.

In nearly every situation, the home sellers that follow the

guidelines in this book, that painstakingly lay out how to prepare, price and position your home in your market, end up selling homes faster and for the most money. You can also download our, How to sell your home for up to 18% more report while you are on our website at: www.kinderreese.com/sellformore.

Here are the three things you should watch out for, when reviewing your estimated proceeds.

First, review the tax prorations. In many cases this is going to be one of the largest items on the closing statement and, depending on closing date, the title company could collect up to 12 months worth of prorated taxes at closing. This comes as a shock to many homeowners, and many agents, in an effort to make the net proceeds look favorable, will neglect to include this on your net sheet. The good news is that if your taxes are up to date or paid out of your mortgage escrow account, you will get a refund of the remaining insurance and taxes that are withheld. This usually is a surprise check you get in the mail, 1 to 2 weeks after the closing, from your mortgage escrow withholdings. Be sure to double-check these figures at closing.

Second, be careful of what you agree to if paying a portion of the buyer's closing costs. Different loans require different loan closing costs to be paid by the seller. This is most common in FHA or VA loans. If you agree to pay any portion of the buyer's closing costs, always cap that number, i.e., "not to exceed $X." This will keep you from getting stuck paying lender fees or origination costs that are out of the ordinary.

Lastly, the biggest threat to your wallet is related to repairs. This is the biggest negotiating mistake that is made when an offer is presented, and should be factored into your estimate as well. The buyer's offer will most likely have an amount for repairs, and that amount can usually be any number you can dream of. I've seen it be anywhere between $500 and $10,000. This means that you, the seller, would be obligated during the inspection option period, for repairs up to that amount. If the home inspector finds issues exceeding that amount, you are officially out of contract and renegotiation begins. The buyer has the upper hand here. You already agreed to your best offer and now the buyer can come back and ask you to do more than you originally agreed. Ouch!

You should consider doing a sellers home inspection that you can use to attract a higher offer, instead of giving the buyer the upper hand in the negotiation. This method is not common practice for all real estate agents, so be sure to ask them to show you their process to avoid pitfalls, and help extract the most money from your home sale.

About Michael and Jay

More than ten years ago, Jay Kinder and Michael Reese inadvertently caught up with each other one summer afternoon at Lake Texoma. Real estate was the discussion of the day as a young Jay Kinder shared how he sold 233 homes the previous year to a very open-minded Michael Reese. Who knew that a chance encounter would turn into the wildly successful partnership that is now Kinder Reese Real Estate Advisors?

Since that day, Michael, Jay and their teams have sold more than 4,250 homes combined. Together, they've brought in more than $18,000,000 in commissions for their real estate businesses, and haven't looked back since that fateful day.

Both Jay and Michael have been members of *Realtor Magazine*'s prestigious "30 under 30" group. They have also both been ranked within the Top 100 of the 400 most successful real estate teams in North America by Real Trends of *The Wall Street Journal*.

Individually, Jay has established himself as one of the top agents in the world, selling more than 3,000 homes while capturing 14% market share in Lawton, Oklahoma. In 2007, Jay was named #2 in the World for Coldwell Banker, competing with over 120,000 realtors – being the youngest to ever obtain this achievement. The results don't stop there. In 2007, Jay was also ranked #1 in Oklahoma and #2 in the Southern Region including over 1,700 realtors from 14 states. He has been recognized with the honor of #1 Sales Associate in Oklahoma in 2002-2010 before opening his new company, Jay Kinder Real Estate Experts in 2011.

Michael has also enjoyed immense success as one of Keller Williams' top 50 agents worldwide. He is regularly ranked as one of the Top 5 teams in the Southwest Region for Keller Williams, and he and his team recently broke the record for buyer sales for the Keller Williams he worked out of in Frisco, Texas – before going independent as the Michael Reese Home Selling Team. Michael earned $1,000,000 in GCI after only his sixth year in the business and he's never made less since then.

In 2004, Jay and Michael started Kinder Reese Real Estate Partners with the aim of helping success-minded agents like themselves create the business and lifestyle that virtually every real estate agent dreams about. Kinder Reese currently serves more than 23,000 agents across North America with its revolutionary business model and innovative business systems.

In 2011, they co-founded the National Association of Expert Advisors®(NAEA), which offers the most prestigious designations that a real estate agent in today's market can have. The Certified Home Selling Advisor® designee has been recognized as an agent with a highly differentiated, proven, repeatable system to get sellers up to 18% more than the methods of average real estate agents. The NAEA's goal is to provide the highest level of education, training and business materials to agents who are truly serious about bringing the absolute best consumer experience to today's home sellers and buyers.

The Certified Home Selling Advisor® designation is a four-part certification process that helps today's real estate agents learn what they need to truly distinguish themselves from their competition and establish themselves as the true, number one choice for real estate consumers in their marketplace.

They are both best-selling authors on Amazon's Top Ten list of books for small businesses with their book *Trendsetters*, and they can be seen on NBC, ABC, CBS, CNBC and other major networks as Expert Advisors™ on the television show, *The New Masters of Real Estate.*

Currently, Jay lives in Frisco, Texas with his wife, Amber, and has three sons, Brayden, Karsen and Riggs. Michael lives in Frisco, Texas with his wife Stacey and their two sons, Cache and Crew.

CHAPTER 3

THE CASH FLOW JOURNEY

BY MIKE CONLON

I remember how excited I was back in early 2002 when a friend gave me a copy of Robert Kyosaki's, *Rich Dad Poor Dad* book. At the time, I was making a very good living running a large, financial planning firm, but I was also working 60+ hours/week and the business was very unfulfilling. Kyosaki's book talked about two great real estate concepts that I wasn't familiar with – depreciation (taking non-cash deductions over a number of years – great tax deferral) and passive income (making money while you sleep). His book made investing in commercial real estate, primarily apartment buildings, seem relatively easy. You do your research, try to buy at a price below the current market rates, and start collecting checks. Even though I had zero real estate experience at the time, I was "gung ho" to jump into the real estate game. I wanted to start my cash flow journey and my initial goal was to get a minimum of $10,000/month in passive cash flow, add in tax benefits generated from depreciation, and allow myself to work less and enjoy life more.

My first deal was an 8-unit apartment complex in Neenah, WI that I bought for $300,000. I owned the property for 12 months, but I could never get it to cash flow. It seemed that an unexpected maintenance issue always popped up—a broken pipe, worn our air conditioner, broken stove, etc. I sold it for $305,000, which allowed me to break even on the deal. The problem was, my next two deals (4 units and 24 units) I did that year went the same way – they looked good on paper, but an unforeseen expense always popped up and I could never get the deals to be cash flow positive. I really liked the commercial real estate business, but I was getting frustrated, so I knew I had to re-analyze my current system. My analysis led me to the following conclusions:

1. **Only buy commercial real estate in a larger metro area (200,000+ in population) that is growing.** Bigger, faster growing metro areas are better for commercial real estate because they have more employment opportunities for potential residents and/or leasing opportunities. My first few deals were bought in Appleton/Neenah Wisconsin, which has a population under 100,000 and little growth. The Western and Southeastern U.S. have more potential in my opinion than the upper Midwest and Northeast.

2. **Know when to cut your losses.** When do you cut your losses on a bad deal? My gut instinct is that if a property underperforms my initial projections by 25% or more within 12-18 months, even if it is marginally profitable, I am looking to sell it. Always remember that there is another deal out there and most investors make better purchases as they get more experience.

3. **In commercial real estate, bigger is better.** I realized that the small projects I was buying were problematic for creating long-term passive income because a minor unexpected repair or maintenance expense made a significant dent in my monthly cash flow. I think smaller properties (50 units and under) should be held by individuals not looking for a lot of cash flow (i.e., a 401(k) alternative) or to be flipped for a profit to allow you to buy a larger property in the future.

So, I took action and I sold my financial planning business and all three properties in Wisconsin and moved to Orlando, FL in early 2003 and went into the real estate game full time. It was a big change, but Orlando was a much bigger metro area and it was just starting one of its upswings. The first property I bought was a 90-unit apartment building that seemed to be in a good location. I was a little over my head in this new market and made a ton of mistakes with this first property, but it cash flowed about $7,500/month even with a bunch of unexpected cap. ex./maintenance repairs. The first 12 months were pretty good, then the hurricanes hit central Florida in 2004. We had three in a span of eight weeks and I realized how poorly constructed the buildings were, and the two key mistakes I had made – (1) buying a property with a flat roof in Florida (too much rain) and (2) one without cement block on the first floor. I needed to sell. Fortunately, Orlando was a hot market and I had plenty of out-of-state buyers who were as unfamiliar with the market as I was. I had a sale in place quickly for $300,000 more than I bought it for. My real estate investment career was looking up.

But my inexperience came back to bite me again. I put a nice 120-unit apartment complex under contract with the intent of using the proceeds of the sale from the first property, about $900,000, to fund the purchase. I spaced the purchase out about 25 days apart to seemingly give me ample time to close on the sale. The problem came when my Buyer started delaying closing – the first time was for 15 days. At the end of the 15 days, he requested a 20-day extension. I was stuck. I couldn't start over with another buyer and I had $200,000 of non-refundable deposit money at stake in the purchase if I didn't close on time. The Seller in that deal was a big REIT that wasn't willing to give me an extension. When I didn't think things could get worse, about five days into the second extension period, I was at my property and I saw smoke come billowing out of one of the units. Thankfully, no one was hurt, but the unit was a total loss – the pressure was on. Over the next week, I scrambled together a rehab crew and got the fire unit in reasonable shape. I also begged the bank I was working with to give me a two-week unsecured loan for $900,000. After much pleading, they came through with the money and I got my new deal purchased, and a week later got my first property sold. A very stressful period, but I learned a ton.

So, once I had my first win (positive cash flow every month plus a $300,000 gain in 18 months), I started to feel like my decision to go full-time in commercial real estate was a good one. And over the 3½ years in lived in Orlando, I bought 8 mid-size (64-120 units) apartment deals. I was cash flowing over $20,000/month and things were good. Then, in 2006, prices went through the roof in Orlando. A good friend of mine and a great commercial real estate broker, Enon Winkler, brought me unsolicited offers for a couple of my deals. The prices offered were home run prices, but at first I resisted the change that was happening. What would I do with the proceeds? Where would I reinvest? Enon finally talked some sense into me and got me to agree to the sales. I made $1.5 million from one property that I owned for 18 months, $900,000 from another, etc. Of the 8 deals I sold, 7 went into foreclosure within 36 months of the sale date because the new buyers overpaid. The experience in Orlando really reinforced three major rules of real estate that I will never forget:

1. **You make your money in real estate at the purchase:** You need to do an intensive study of the market and buy as far below market as possible. This takes a lot of work, but a knowledgeable broker is a big help. If you buy right, it allows you to ride through a down-turn without having to sell.

2. **Cash Flow is King:** I never buy properties that don't have positive cash flow from day one. You never want to be in a negative cash flow situation in any deal, especially at the start. My job as a good real estate investor is to have a plan in place where I can greatly increase the cash flow in the first 12-18 months either through rent raises, better marketing of vacant units or spaces, and rehabbing vacant units.

3. **Understand the real estate cycles:** I have been through

two up cycles and one down cycle in my real estate career. The real estate cycle in the U.S. over the last 35 years seems to follow this pattern: slow to moderate growth and lending for 4 to 5 years, then a loosening of the lending culture and an explosion of deals for 3 years and especially the last 12 months, ending with a nasty real estate recession that lasts 2 years. The bottom of the recession is obviously the best time to buy. You also learn far more from a down cycle than an up cycle. In early 2017, it seems like we are late in the up cycle.

So, once I sold all of my apartments, I was almost starting all over. In early 2005, I saw an article proclaiming investing in mobile home parks was easier than apartments and provided more cash flow. I had never even driven through a park before, but I was intrigued, so I did a ton of research. I'll never forget visiting with one park owner in Central Florida that had his park for sale. My COO, Chris Barry, and I drove into this 75-space park in a more rural area and noticed it was pretty full with older homes and definitely nothing great. When we got to the back of the park, where the owner lived, we noticed a nice home that had a nice boat and a big, newer RV. The owner was in his early 60's at the time and was very friendly. He told us how he never graduated high school, but cobbled together enough money to buy this park 25 years ago. He said the business had been very good to him. He even showed us three large safes, each about 6 feet high, that were in the back of his house. Each one was filled with cash! Chris and I said to each other on the way out – if this guy is successful in the mobile home park business, surely we can be as well.

So I decided to buy a mobile home park in late 2005 in Lakeland, FL. It was 80 homes on 4 acres – ridiculously tight. This park wasn't great, but it cash flowed nicely each month and Chris felt it was much easier to manage than an apartment complex primarily because we didn't require any maintenance men. Almost all the residents owned their homes and were responsible for their own maintenance. We just "rented the dirt."

So I made the second big pivot in my career. I switched exclusively to buying mobile home parks in 2006 after we sold all the apartments. Because prices for everything were too high in Florida, I had to look at other markets and settled on North Carolina as our new home. We bought 5 larger parks (150 – 225 spaces) in North Carolina between 2006 and 2009. Our initial thoughts proved correct as the parks were much easier to manage and had more cash flow than apartments because of the lower maintenance costs. Plus, at the time, mobile home parks were the "ugly step child" of the real estate industry, so there wasn't the competition for them that there is today. Life was back to normal. I was cash flowing over $25,000/month and working about 20 hours per week.

But in 2011, I started to hear rumblings in the mobile home park industry that a lot of foreclosed deals from 2009-10 would be hitting the market in 2012. So in another big pivot, and a huge leap of faith, I sold all five parks in late 2011 for a very nice profit and got "cash-heavy" waiting for the foreclosed deals to hit the market. But I waited six long months, without cash flow, until mid-2012 when the first deals hit. Then I started buying foreclosed mobile home parks all over the East Coast. For example, we bought two parks in Birmingham, AL, a combined 190 spaces, for $850,000 in early 2013 that were recently appraised for $4 million. In the last four years, I have bought 46 mobile home parks. As of early 2017, I still own 30+ parks with my cash flow now exceeding $100,000/month and a net worth over $25 million. I sold 16 of the parks (my smaller parks with weaker locations) in the last 15 months as prices have risen to all-time highs again, generating profits of over $10 million.

Looking back over the last fifteen years, here are three more big lessons I have learned that I can pass on to new real estate investors:

1. **Your first two years will be your hardest.** Looking back, the first two years are the hardest time to be a real estate investor because you make so many mistakes. I made almost every one in the book. But if you have enough determination and fortitude to make it through the first two years, real estate investing is a fantastic journey and can be quite lucrative.

2. **Ongoing operations are as important as acquisitions.** Buying and selling deals are the fun part about real estate. Ongoing operations, such as repairs and maintenance, cap ex, collecting rent, etc., are just as key to a successful deal, but not nearly as much fun. Kyosaki's books barely mention the operations of properties. Operations are hard, grinding work, but they are vital for having strong cash flow. The problem is that the personality traits required to be successful at acquisitions are almost the exact opposite of those needed to be successful at Operations. The best thing I ever did was bring my current COO, Chris Barry, into my business 15 years ago to run operations. He has a much different skill set than I have and he does a great job!

3. **Reinvest in Your Properties.** Do not get greedy and take all the profits from your properties. I reinvest $500,000 plus per year in my properties with new homes, paved roads, new mailboxes, etc. Reinvesting not only keeps your values up, but it also allows you to raise rents and get more qualified residents.

4. **Change is going to happen – get used to it!** The investment arena is changing faster than ever. In my 15 years in the business, the amount of change is staggering. A good entrepreneur tries to anticipate change the best they can by being very aware (I am a voracious reader) of industry, political, and monetary (interest rate) changes. The more experienced you become, the better you get at anticipating change.

I have made three major changes in 15 years – moving from Wisconsin to Florida; selling all of my apartment complexes and buying into mobile home parks; and then selling all 5 parks in 2011 to take advantage of distressed deals. All changes were scary at first, but I felt in my gut it was the right thing to do at the time. It's all been a part of my Cash Flow Journey. I am incredibly blessed and thankful for all those who have helped me. I can't wait to see where the Journey takes me in the next 15 years!

About Mike

Mike Conlon is President and CEO of Affordable Communities Group, LLC (acgmhc.com) based in Cary, NC. He currently owns 30 mobile home communities with approximately 4,000 spaces in the Midwest and Southeastern U.S. In addition, from 2002 until today, Mike has done 8 full-cycle (buy, rehab, sell) apartment deals and 16 full-cycle mobile home park deals, generating profits of over $20 million.

Mike is also a best-selling author of two books – *Unconventional Wealth* and *Transform* (both available on Amazon) and has been seen on ABC, CBS, NBC, CNBC, Fox, *The Wall Street Journal* and several other publications.

Mike is originally from Green Bay, WI (go Pack!). He received his law degree from the University of Minnesota in 1990. He was active in the financial planning business from 1990 through 2002 where he owned a financial planning broker-dealer that he grew from $1.6 million in revenue to over $40 million in five years, and then sold to a large national insurance company. He also owned a large, full-service financial planning firm that had over $100 million in client assets, which he sold in late 2002.

Mike can be reached at:

- mconlon1@gmail.com.
- www.mikeconlon.com
- www.acgmhc.com

CHAPTER 4

SEEKING OUT THE AMERICAN DREAM—

IMMIGRANTS FINDING HOME OWNERSHIP IN THE LAND OF OPPORTUNITY

BY RAÚL ARRIAGA

I truly believe that home ownership is the symbol of the American dream; the cornerstone of realizing something wonderful.

I have a passionate heart about helping immigrants find the one thing in America that people worldwide envy most, although it isn't always easily recognized by those who were born here. What I'm referring to is the dream of home ownership. It is such an empowering concept and one that drives people to work hard to achieve it. My experiences have taught me that through acknowledging and assisting those who seek this, a great many dreams can be realized for individuals, as well as their families. There are those pivotal times in life when it takes not having something to realize just how special it is.

My parents were immigrants and I was born in the U.S.A. However, at the age of two, my father moved us back to Mexico to retire and raise his family of nine children there. By the age of sixteen, I was back in the United States, hoping to achieve my own successes and gain opportunities for my "big break." I lived with my siblings and our conditions were humble, a mobile home that our large family filled. Yes, it was just a bit crowded, but there is one thing you cannot crowd out—opportunity to move up and along. It just takes hard work, or at least not fearing the possibility of having to do it.

As a young man, I looked around me and didn't see what I did not have. I saw the potential for opportunities that I knew did not exist for me, personally, in Mexico. It was up to me to act on and take these moments to make my life better. So, I began to work, and worked hard. I started in the retail industry, but it wasn't where I envisioned that I could be. I knew there was something else waiting for me. Finally, upon the advice of my older sister, I entered into real estate. It changed everything in my life and helped me hone in on what would become my life's passion. This passion is helping immigrants recognize the empowerment that stems from owning real estate in the United States, as it is an experience that doesn't seem to be replicated anywhere else in the world, and it is amazing.

AN UNDERSERVED MARKET

People come to America to make a better life, and I am so excited to be a part of that dream.

Although I was born a U.S. citizen, I saw an immediate market that I could serve in the real estate industry. That was the underserved market of the immigrants coming to the United States. I saw these spirited and incredible people with endless potential. But even more so, I saw an invaluable opportunity to educate people on the value that immigrants bring to the communities they live in. Far more common than the bad stories that receive much publicity, are the good stories of people with heart, skills, and a genuine love of the United States. These are the stories of success and inspiration that were the backbone of those immigrants who founded America, and these same principles still exist in most people who wish to come to the United States today. It's truly amazing, and to work with people like this and learn their stories makes me a blessed man.

The way many people visualize an immigrant is someone of little to no means, coming to a new country in order to pursue a better life. This is certainly one type of immigrant, and these people can rise to do amazing things in their lives and stand strongly for their adopted countries. However, there is another immigrant, and this person is one that has clout, prestige, and resources in their home country. But they also recognize the power of what a life in the United States can bring them. The value these people bring to the United States when they come here is good for everybody and includes:

- Investing in new business and commerce: these can be both expansions of businesses into the U.S. and also start-up businesses. These investors and entrepreneurs take advantage of EB-5 visas to bring value with them. These are visas that allow a foreign-born person to live in the United States if they commit one-million-dollars to a business, and hire ten employees, or else commit five-hundred-thousand-dollars to a business in an urban revival district, and hire at least five employees.
- Creating new jobs: there's few greater places to grow a business than in the United States. These jobs and companies that may start small, often grow big because of the skill sets and talents of their CEOs and the entrepreneurial mindset of those who run them. Those five or ten jobs can often keep sprouting to sustainable, vibrant small-to-medium sized businesses that change lives of everyone in a community for the better. Those who appreciate what they have received are often the greatest advocates of paying these rewards

forward in their communities.
- Urban renewal initiatives: there are growth initiatives and incentives for areas that are in need of urban renewal. These places are often overlooked by those investors and entrepreneurs that are born in the United States, but they are appealing areas of opportunity for immigrants. These immigrant business people are glad to bring opportunities for others with them, along with their message of hope for renewal.

Back in 2013, I was interviewed for a *Time Magazine* article titled: *The New — and Rich — Immigrants from Mexico: How Their Money is Changing Texas*. In this article, I stated, "It's not the same migration we're used to seeing, low-income families migrating to the US, undocumented, looking for any type of job. They are well-educated, they have money, they come here with EB-5 visas." With immigrants from Mexico and other Spanish-speaking countries, specifically, how often do we think of doctors, lawyers, top-level executives, and other elite professionals wanting to come to the U.S.A.? This important and dynamic sector often gets overlooked. Well, with the results they are bringing, people are looking now. And this is what excites me. The potential is limitless. Being a part of it inspires me to give my best every day and never stop my own pursuits of growth and knowledge.

THE APPEAL OF THE AMERICAN REAL ESTATE MARKET

"You see, without hard work and responsibility, there is no American Dream. Hard work lays the foundation. Our solidarity makes work pay, for all of us. For the greater good. That's what our vision of shared prosperity is all about."
~ Florence King

I work with immigrants from across the world, but due to

being bilingual in Spanish and English, the Spanish-speaking community is a natural fit for me. As a business man, I understand their professional needs, and as a man who went through the process of achieving property ownership, I relate to their driving and compelling desires to achieve this in the United States, as it is so very special.

The NAFTA (North America Free Trade Agreement) office in Mexico City hires me every year to give tours for a group of forty to fifty entrepreneurs who are looking at investing in the United States. These are people who have money and resources. They come to visit me in Texas and we tour properties and I help educate them on how the process works. The needs of these individuals vary and they look for a variety of types of real estate, including:

- Commercial properties
- Primary residences
- Second homes (vacation homes)
- Investment properties

Being the one to connect their dreams to the resources is endlessly inspiring to me. You cannot beat the feelings of contribution that stem from working in a service industry and seeing the results of your efforts. It's all-encompassing in a healthy real estate practice.

Many people do not realize that these immigrants do have a life in Mexico or their home country. They don't look to move to avoid oppression or persecution. They are business people. And like all creative and business-minded individuals, they have strict criteria on how they invest their monies. It has to be in something solid. And even with the shake-ups the U.S. real estate market has on occasion, even on its worst day, it is relatively solid. In Mexico, the peso is so volatile that it isn't a great option, not when compared to the U.S. dollar.

CALCULATED RISK IS NOTHING NEW TO ANY INVESTOR AND THE U.S. OFFERS A PLETHORA OF OPPORTUNITIES FOR SMART RISK

As our world keeps changing, many times we may feel further disconnected from each other than we ever have been before. Through what I do, I feel excitement for the chances to help bridge those gaps that may hinder people from connecting with their dreams. Staying up-to-speed on the international market and how I can best participate in it and look out for my clients' best interests, is always at the heart of what I do and in my mind. Designations such as that of CIPS (Certified International Property Specialist) have given me the access to additional resources, trends, and valuable data that help me to keep being an effective and relevant advocate for people who wish to own real estate in the United States and abroad. People's dreams are not taken lightly by me, and knowing that I can participate is a great honor.

OUR BRIGHTEST DAYS ARE AHEAD

It's not just a transaction, it's a source of pride and accomplishment too.

When people use my team to view and purchase property, they are using a group of people vested in their dream. We know the process, both in America and in a great many other countries, and this benefits them greatly. It's relatable, understandable, and streamlined in a way to help them have an optimal experience with us.

Sharing in this journey and seeing that awe-inspired look that both business people and homeowners have when they see that deed with their name on it is impressionable. It fuels the drive to keep cultivating this amazing opportunity for as many people as we can.

This is so personal for me and I put all my efforts and expertise into making sure that my clients get the best deals and have access to good resources. All of this enhances their experience and I want it to be nothing short of wonderful. The technology, the communication, the multiple languages, etc. Our goal is to serve people smoothly and exceed expectations. We want to help, regardless of price. If I can't personally do something, I know someone I trust who can.

All of this is designed around one thing: letting people realize they can have this wonderful American dream, too! It's not a dream for one, but a dream for many.

About Raul

Raúl Arriaga brings a unique perspective to his thriving real estate career. As someone who has seen the value of achieving the American dream of home ownership through life's experiences and helping clients, he has taken this passion to the people and is in the top 1% of producers in the Dallas/Ft. Worth area he serves. Today, he runs the Arriaga Group, which he founded in 2012 and has helped hundreds of clients since this time.

There is a wide variety of individuals that Raúl works with locally and internationally, including diplomats, entrepreneurs, executives, athletes, business owners, organizations, and individual families. He helps them secure real estate that meets their specific needs, large or small. Being bilingual is also helpful. Raúl is fluent in Spanish and English. His extensive designations lend to his expertise and include: CIPS (Certified International Property Specialist), SRS (Seller Representative Specialist), ALHS (Accredited Luxury Home Specialist), ABR (Accredited Buyer Representation), TRC (Transnational Referral Certification) and I.R.E.S. (International Real Estate Specialist). Raùl is also an active with NAHREP (North Texas) AEM, (Association of Mexican Entrepreneurs), where he serves as a board member.

Raúl is a sought-out expert in his field, having been quoted extensively for his expert opinion and experiences. He's also a published author, having released the book, *The Ultimate Guide to Dallas Real Estate*, in 2014. Now he's also a co-author who has contributed a chapter in the exciting book *Real Estate GameChangers*. According to Raúl, "These opportunities to reach out to people internationally and show them the unique opportunities that exist for people from all countries in America's real estate market is one I appreciate. I'm so passionate about this and always welcome an opportunity to engage with a diverse group of immigrants who have an opportunity for something more in America. These are established and skilled people much of the time."

Everything Raúl accomplishes takes hard work, and he had no better role model to show bravery and resilience than his mother, Audelia. Raising nine children in the U.S. and Mexico, hoping for them to have the best opportunities, wasn't always easy. But according to Raúl, "She is the hardest working woman I have ever known and will ever know." Raúl doesn't take anything for granted, from his clients to his son Maximo. Opportunities to help exist everywhere. One of his favorite involvements is mentoring ESL (English as a Second Language) students, helping them complete high school and consider pursuing higher education. He is also actively involved in the community, helping new immigrants better understand and integrate into their new communities through social, cultural, and educational events.

In his free time, Raúl loves traveling and experiencing different cultures. He's an avid follower of Formula 1 racing, passionate about soccer, enjoys extreme sports, plus watching professional sports, working out, and reading anything that helps him grow as a person and enhances his life.

Connect with Raúl Arriaga at:

- Website: www.YourDallasHomesGuide.com
- Email: Raul@RaulArriaga.com or call 214.682.4498
- LinkedIn: http://www.linkedin.com/in/RaulArriagaRealtor
- Facebook: https://www.facebook.com/DFWLuxuryHomes
- Twitter: http://twitter.com/RaulArriaga

CHAPTER 5

WHEN AVERAGE JUST WON'T DO...

FINDING THE BEST REALTOR® TO HELP YOU BUY A HOME

BY KATHLEEN FORREST,
Branch Owner & Broker

Why is it so easy for some of us to choose "the best" for some things and then disregard the value of that for others? Human nature, I suppose. How many of you would choose to have a neighbor, friend, or relative perform a surgery on you because they'll give you a deal? How about if you have to go to court for something? Settling for an attorney that practices law on a part-time basis might not be such a good idea. For life's most important moments, you want proven professionals who are at the top of their field. Nothing else makes sense. These same expectations of professionalism should exist for any Realtor® you choose to work with to purchase a property – especially if you plan on calling it "home."

The skills and proven stellar results of a Realtor® are directly proportionate to what your purchasing experience will be.

Buying a new home is so exciting! It's a part of the American dream that drives and compels people to succeed in life just so they can experience home ownership. There is no more logical, desirable, or greater reward to your life's most incredible moments, such as graduating college, landing an exciting job opportunity, and even getting married and beginning a new life with "the one."

Let's not forget the changes that take place in our lives as we move along, either! Kids leave home and downsizing is necessary, just as much as families merge and find a need to upsize. Then you go into the maintenance of a home. Do you want maintenance-free or are you the one who looks forward to riding your lawnmower across your sprawling acres? These decisions are important and easier to determine with the right Realtor® working by your side, helping break down the entire process. As a consumer, you really need to understand your needs vs. desires. I call this "The Why". Sometimes we clearly know our "why", and other times people need to really bounce their thoughts and ideas off a professional. This is where I come in, and this is where I've created a noticeable gap from the way I conduct business compared to the "average old process."

The Buyer's Interview

With a thorough and thoughtful opportunity to communicate, "The Why" is easier to determine. A positive experience begins and customers know that I am vested in their needs.

Without exception, I do a buyer's interview to get to know my clients and their needs thoroughly. It's an invaluable opportunity to better understand their style preferences, where they struggle, where they are uncertain, and where I can help educate them. This is where a game plan is created and meaningful, and forward-moving actions can take place. The best part is that we are doing this together, on the same page and really working as a team for their goals. It's not about me and my opinions; it's about clients and their needs. Have you ever been in one of those situations where you are across from someone that is trying to talk you into something more than educate you? You feel like you're the target of that "used car salesman" cliché. What you really want doesn't matter, only the commission. Every horror you can think of is pretty much the opposite of my goals for a real estate experience with me. I value buyer's interviews greatly, because the time invested aligns us, allowing for a smoother, more rewarding transaction.

It all comes down to preparation and execution.

If you want the best, what should you look for and expect from a Realtor®? This is what I am sharing with you. It's this insight that allows me to get reviews such as this recent Zillow review: "Phenomenal experience! Kathleen is very professional and knowledgeable. She went out of her way to ensure our house-buying experience was the best it could have been. Very dedicated. Although professional, she also worked with my family on a personal level. We hope to stay in touch with her, and we give her and her team the highest recommendation possible!"

Smart Strategies for Buyers to Find the Best Realtor®

Buyers should never leave a meeting with a Realtor® without feeling confident that all their questions and concerns have been answered, as well as their needs met.

There is a lot to consider when hiring a Realtor®, but as a prepared consumer you can learn a lot quickly. Here's some insight into the questions and knowledge that a top-level Realtor® can easily discuss with you and by giving factual information more than personal opinion.

1. **The resume and credentials.**
   A resume reveals wonders about a person. Every professional should have one and if they don't, it's like the yellow caution flag at the Indy 500, warning you to slow down and assess the risk. For a Realtor® the resume includes valuable information such as:
   - where they have worked and length of experience
   - their strengths, skills, and specialties
   - what credentials they've earned and how often they advance their education in the real estate industry
   - referrals from past clients that speak about their experiences

2. **A clearly-stated plan of action.**
   When you are purchasing a home, timelines and expectations matter. To gain a greater understanding of what the process will entail—because it is complex—the best Realtors® offer a clearly-stated plan of action. This allows you to better understand the entire process, which includes:
   - preapprovals and approvals
   - home searches and a book specific to tracking properties
   - contracts and addendums
   - earnest money, down payment, and closing costs
   - housing payments, including principle and interest, taxes, insurance, and possibly PMI (private mortgage insurance)
   - property inspections, termite inspections, appraisals, and the final walk-through
   - the closing day expectations and experience

It is important to know what all these steps are, how long they take, and why they are important to your experience. You don't cut corners when purchasing a home!

3. **The differences and distinctions of the Realtor®.**
   You don't have to have the IQ of a rocket scientist to get

a license and call yourself a Realtor®! The best Realtors® know this and they go the distance to set themselves apart and create distinction from those less committed. This is one thing that I've always strived to do and it has set me apart. It's about more than showing homes, it's about offering viable solutions that are in the best interests of buyers. Ask any Realtor® you interview about:

- Grants and free money: there are many programs out there that can offer assistance in down payments, closing costs, and all with no recapture tax (a tax you pay if you refinance or sell within a certain period of time). Recently I found a program where a buyer using a VA/zero-down loan also got a grant, handing them 3.5% of the purchase price on the home they were buying ($5,250 on a $150,000 home) which offset the VA funding fee and paid down their initial mortgage balance. My advice: don't box yourself in and limit your options or make assumptions about what you may, or may not, qualify for.
- Home warranties: the term "home warranty" offers a certain level of comfort, but not all home warranties are the same. Some options look good, but don't really do anything for you unless it is an extreme situation. Imagine buying the car of your dreams and later finding out it doesn't have an engine. Not good! Your warranty should be set for action, should the need for it arise. Any Realtor® representing you should be able to tell you the pros and cons of any home warranty from any company offering it. Additionally, you need to be aware of the benefits and values of having an extended warranty in place for new home construction. Most people get a standard one-year builder warranty, but buyers can negotiate an extended warranty that covers appliances, electrical, plumbing, HVAC, and the house from top to bottom for an additional four years. There's no substitute for peace of mind with your home. Why

spend money on repairs to your new home instead of filling it with the things that make it a special place for you and yours?

- Punch lists: buyers who are interested in purchasing new homes need a punch list! This is the document that helps ensure that the home is truly ready to move into—even after the builder says it is. It addresses everything in the home from top to bottom, including cracks, flawed craftsmanship, incomplete work, leaks in windows, etc. I have yet to have a buyer who inspects their new home and has no punch list. For example, I just had buyers that were told by a builder their property was complete and move-in ready. I found two plus pages of items for the builder to correct that the buyer had not noticed, and the builder certainly wasn't going to point out to the buyers.
- Inspections: not all inspectors are the same! Most inspectors specialize in different types of properties. For example, it takes a different set of skills to inspect an old home, compared to a new construction or a historic property. You want the eyes that are looking at your purchase to be seeing what they have to with great wisdom and 20/20 vision. This is no time to learn the hard lessons of hindsight! The cheapest and most quickly available inspector isn't always the best. It reminds me of the difference between the "snip and clip is us" salon that offers cheap walk-in haircuts compared to the "hair mastery is us" service you wait a few weeks for. With "snip and clip", if something goes wrong you quickly realize that it would have been better to wait two weeks for a good cut compared to that three months it takes your 'hack' job to grow back.
- Closing day: this is the day where that home you've emotionally and mentally placed yourself in becomes yours. Having it be a day of celebration and a smooth transaction is your sweet reward. Chaos and confusion shouldn't exist. But how? Through your Realtor®!

Janet Jackson once asked, "What have you done for me lately?" Don't hold back on asking your Realtor® this same question. They need to be there for you and looking out for your best interests on this important day. Were all your seller-paid closing costs credited? Were the taxes prorated accurately? And, believe it or not, does the Realtor® you are considering even attend the closing is a question you should ask. If they don't, press the shiny, red button that ends your interview with them.

A lot happens at closing, and their service to you should include being there through the entire process, as much or as little as you feel they should be. I can tell you this from personal experience—I'm yet to meet a client who doesn't want me there. By this point we're close, a family looking out for each other. Also, I'm ready to celebrate the exciting moment my clients are having!

4. **Define the levels and methods of communication.** Personally, I cannot imagine not having the highest levels of streamlined communication in any transaction I am involved in. This is with the buyers, as well as any other agents or entities that have an impact on the transaction. As a buyer, you need to be comfortable stating how often you wish to be communicated with. You should expect:
    - updates on all facets of your transaction as they happen.
    - communication to be had when a Realtor® tells you they are going to provide it.

The way I help buyers understand what is going on and when they definitely will hear from me or my team is by providing a checklist. Behind the scenes, there are a great many people working to make their transaction run smoothly, too! Truly, our buyers are the stars on our real estate walk of fame!

5. **The team approach makes for a stronger buyer experience.** A team working for you is of great value, bringing you assurance that every detail of your transaction is being

addressed. Oversights are unacceptable. As mentioned earlier, the team takes care of all the things behind the scenes that are important to your transaction. And better yet, the team member is working in an area that is their strength. Think of a computer and how it works. Most of us don't know how…we just want it to work. The real estate team working for you is the circuit board, hard drive, and surge protectors that protect you, working efficiently and fluidly on your behalf. For you, it just clicks. The team works with seller's agents, title companies, keeps in touch with your lender, plus converses and coordinates with appraisers, inspectors, and any other entities playing a role in your transaction. You're busy, and knowing that a team working for you is smart, efficient, looking out for your best interests, and specially trained in their area of expertise, should be a non-negotiable. It saves on surprises and enhances the entire, exciting experience.

6. **Your tiger in the jungle.**
   I pride myself on being personable and aggressive; tenacious yet courteous. You don't need an agent that is so sweet everyone loves them, yet you also don't want one that thinks it is optimal to yell and cause a ruckus in order to negotiate the best terms for a buyer. Think of Teddy Roosevelt's famous line, "Walk softly and carry a big stick." Being abrasive in negotiations can be costly—mostly for you, the buyer. Finesse, assertiveness, poise, and professionalism can be displayed while still getting you a deal that's sweet… totally!

MY PLEDGE TO MY CLIENTS

Going beyond the "must do" elements of a transaction and into the "want to do" steps that reveal your passion for real estate, is a source of personal joy for me.

I've just shared a lot of information with you, but I have just scratched the surface. Real estate is constantly evolving due to regulations, changing markets and trends, and exciting new concepts. Professionally, keeping up on these things is a must.

But let's get personal.

For me, I know that my team and I have the details covered. It's the small extras that have really proven to add a lot to my transactions:

- going out of your way to accommodate someone's schedule or needs.
- thoughtful gestures that show you relate to and "get" your buyers' busy lives.
- being a caring and genuinely committed partner in a buyer's transaction gives me the drive and energy to work at a high level.

Nothing beats the personal touch and connection that I have with my clients. They become friends. I know them and I care about what's happening in their lives. They know it's sincere. I truly feel that this is why over 90% of my business comes from referrals. This is the one statistic, aside from sales records, that really speaks volumes about what my team and I offer. We are willing to work to be the best. And that is always working for you!

About Kathleen

Kathleen Forrest is the Branch Owner and Broker for Metro Brokers of Oklahoma. She specializes in residential property sales and is the #1 Individual Buyer's Agent in Oklahoma for three years running. From her humble beginnings working in a farming community, she has a matchless work ethic which she uses to guide her success through her many endeavors.

A lover of education, Kathleen has earned two Bachelor's Degrees and a Master's Degree. She's worked as a teacher and advocate for special needs individuals and this is where she got her first taste of real estate. In attempts to get the state to recognize that many of these people were good candidates for home ownership, rather than just renting, she was told she would need to get a license to fight this battle. Challenge accepted. She did and was able to get a grant passed that gave the potential of home ownership to this group of people.

Later, she did research and found grants to assist single mothers pursuing the American dream of home ownership. The word of Kathleen's passion and commitment to people owning homes was spreading. She was featured on the news and within a few months, hundreds of women lined up to work with Kathleen, looking for what options existed for them to purchase a home.

Today, Kathleen consistently ranks in the top 1% in Oklahoma real estate and is recognized as top 1% by Zillow and Trulia. She's been featured in Top Agent Magazine and also selected as one of the 10 Best In Oklahoma by the American Institute of Real Estate Professionals. Her office has been selected 10 Best In Oklahoma for Customer Satisfaction and she has been recognized by the National Association of Professional Women for six straight years. Other awards include Diamond Club recipient, Master's Club recipient, REAL Trends Top Performer, Helping Hand Award Winner, Centurion Award Winner, 10-Star Award Winner, Keller Williams Quad Gold Award Winner, 5-Star Award for Customer Satisfaction, 7-Star Award for Top Income Achievement, Top Brokerage Award Winner, and more!

In addition to those who live in her market, Kathleen also works with a diverse group of relocation clientele that includes oil/gas workers, Boeing relocations, military relocations, medical relocations, and even international relocations. She is a certified relocation and new construction specialist and has sold nearly $400,000,000 in residential real estate to date.

Kathleen also has a passion for "giving back" and "paying it forward." This began when she formed a school for girls in South America. Impacted by a terrible tragedy in her own family, she also lends vigorous support to domestic abuse victims and has formed a non-profit foundation to assist and protect children and other parties to domestic violence. Currently, she is assisting in the production of a movie based on this plight to bring awareness and raise funds.

Meet Kathleen and learn more about buying or selling in Oklahoma.

- Email: kathleen@kathleenforrest.com
- Cell: 405-476-9600 Office: 405-330-1859
- Facebook: Kathleen Forrest Metro Brokers of Oklahoma
- Website: www.kathleenforrest.com

CHAPTER 6

DON'T EVEN THINK ABOUT HIRING A REAL ESTATE AGENT UNTIL YOU'VE READ THIS CHAPTER. . . TWICE!

BY ADAM STARK

How do you pick the agent that is right for you?

There is a sense of mystery out there concerning how the real estate industry "works." I'd like to shed some light on that. Before giving you my opinion, I'll simply rattle off a list of facts many people don't know about real estate agents and the "business model."

- Real estate agents are usually independent contractors, not employees.
- Most of us work on straight commission. We do not receive a salary.
- Most agents do not receive an advertising allowance, a client entertainment allowance, or an allowance of any kind. We pay for everything out of our own pockets.
- Usually the agent's broker takes a cut of the commission check. It varies from brokerage to brokerage. Sometimes it is a scale that adjusts based on how many homes an agent

has sold throughout the year. For example, the more homes an agent sells, the higher percentage of the commission they keep. This means they make more "profit" (as a percentage of the commission) in the later months of the year. This is true for some, but not all, agents.

- As it is documented in many best-selling personal development books for real estate agents, the easiest way to get rich selling real estate is to get as many listings as possible. (I'll touch on that topic later in the book.) Sometimes this is at odds with what is best for the client.
- Many agents also have to pay a "desk fee" (rent for keeping a desk in an office).
- There will be additional closing costs above and beyond paying the agent's commission. These are always negotiable between the buyer and seller.
- Agents incur a lot more expenses selling a home than most people realize. Just one example is the price of gasoline, and wear and tear on a vehicle. When you're constantly driving to meetings and showing homes, the miles add up pretty quickly! I drive about 30,000 miles a year – assuming I don't take any additional road trips or vacations out of state. It's a pretty major expense!
- According to the National Association of Realtors 2016 Member Survey, the median income for Realtors is $33,500. For the most part, real estate agents are not making big bucks.
- We all have our listings on each other's web sites. The fancy term for this is "Broker Reciprocity."
- Any licensed agent out there can show any company's listings—unless the seller doesn't want it that way (which is rare).
- It will take a few hours for an agent to do the proper research and create what's called a "CMA". A CMA is a report that tells home sellers what their home is worth, and what price it should be listed at. Some agents have fancy software that automatically generates a report by pulling data from the MLS. These automatically-generated reports are usually

very unreliable, as intangibles make a big difference. For this reason, I personally shy away from being overly dependent on software.

- There are lots of weird laws that prohibit agents from giving certain kinds of advice. For example, I am not allowed to tell you if a neighborhood is good or bad. I can't even say things like, "Stay away from that neighborhood, there's a lot of crime there." This is called steering, and is actually illegal according to the Fair Housing Act. "Steering" applies to most qualitative questions: demographics of a neighborhood, quality of the schools, etc. Legally, all I can do is point you to websites that provide objective, hard data. In my humble opinion, this is a really stupid law. I completely understand the intent of the law (preventing agents from discriminating), but it seems a bit silly. If I were a homebuyer from out of town, I would want my agent to tell me their opinion about these topics! I'll probably get in trouble for this little rant, but it's a common complaint amongst real estate agents. Everybody is thinking it, but I'm willing to actually say it: good intentions, dumb law. I have a reputation for being brutally honest, and my clients appreciate that about me. That being said, I'm 99% sure I'll 'catch flack' for expressing my views in this paragraph. But you deserve to know the truth.

Now that you've got a crash course in the "business model" of real estate, let's dive into picking the agent that's right for you.

What I'm about to say might offend some people, but it is what it is:

IF YOU WANT THE BEST SERVICE, HIRE A FULL-TIME AGENT!

It's pretty self-explanatory: full time agents devote their entire day to buying and selling real estate for their clients. It's not a hobby or a part time gig; it's their career. Full-time agents spend at least

40 hours a week serving their clients. I've found it's typically 50 to 60 hours, even up to 70 hours during peak selling season.

Again, to be brutally honest, there is no way a "part-time" agent who is trying to make some extra spending money will have the expertise and knowledge that a full-time agent does. Do you really want to trust the purchase or sale of a $200,000 asset (or a million-dollar asset, for that matter) to someone who is just *dabbling* in real estate?

Full-time agents are immersed daily in the world of real estate. In fact, most full-time agents I know don't even need to do much research to create a "market analysis" for someone wanting to sell their home—after a quick tour, we can quote a pretty accurate listing price. Doing the actual research merely gives us hard data to prove our estimate.

When you spend hours every day checking out the latest listings on the MLS, doing research on behalf of your clients, attending open houses, and researching comparables, it's almost hard not to become an expert on the local real estate market. The problem is that part-time agents aren't doing all of the above, or sometimes, . . . any of the above.

They buy/sell a few properties a year. They're looking to make some extra cash, maybe a take a vacation they couldn't otherwise afford. Perhaps they're retired and just want something to do. Whatever their motivation, you should think long and hard before hiring someone who is "part-time."

From my perspective, the "part-time" trend started in the late 1990's and 2000's as the housing market heated up. During the housing boom, you actually could work part- time and still make $40,000 a year (or more!) as a real estate agent. That's on top of whatever you were earning at your "real job." With today's market, there are many full-time agents earning that much. . . or less. Oh, how times change!

Needless to say, it was crazy. Word soon spread that real estate agents were making a killing (many of us were), and newly-licensed agents started popping up like eager prospectors looking for gold. Houses were selling like hotcakes—it didn't take much skill to show up to closings and sign papers! That may be an oversimplification, but it's not too far from the truth. I think this was a time period when people started to feel like real estate agents were making money *too* easily. And I can't blame them for thinking that. Many homeowners started to silently wonder, "Wait, why am I writing you a commission check for $12,000? You hardly did anything to market it! My home sold in 8 days—that's $1,500 per day!!!"

Today, many homeowners are *still* skeptical about the value provided by a real estate agent (which is why more and more people are trying to sell their home as a "For Sale By Owner"). I think this skepticism is a holdover from the days of the housing boom, when, to be completely honest, *that skepticism was probably justified.*

During the 2000's, it wasn't that hard to make a good living (6 figures or more) as a real estate agent. I personally knew agents that got their license and within two years were making over $100k. Sometimes even in their very first year! There are not many professions where you can be a top income earner after two years on the job—with little to no training.

For a good part of the 2000's, the marketing plan involved three steps:

1. Upload new listing to the MLS
2. Place your sign in the yard
3. Sell it within a few weeks, show up to closing, collect commission check

It's not hard to see why people from all walks of life wanted to get in on the action! You could make millions as a real estate "investor" by simply buying a property in a nice area, holding on to it for a few years, and selling it after it had appreciated by 20%. This involved zero skill. *Anybody* could do it, and many people did. It was like a game of hot potato—you just didn't want to be stuck holding an overvalued asset when the bubble popped. And eventually it did. . .

All good things must come to an end.

Without getting into too much detail, low interest rates driven by the federal government's housing policy created an environment where ***everyone thought houses would keep appreciating at astronomically high rates.***

Historically, real estate appreciates at the rate of inflation or more. If you look at long-term trends, owning a home is not a get-rich-quick scheme. Unless of course, you rode the housing bubble like a surfer. During the 2000's, homes were appreciating at 5-10% annually! It was chaotic. And it created a casino-like approach to buying homes.

Because people irrationally believed that the appreciation was permanent and their home would continue to increase in value by 5-10% annually, they rushed to get HELOs (home equity lines of credit) to borrow against their equity. ***In a nutshell, people were using their homes as ATM's.*** They used this money to go out and buy consumer products like boats, fancy cars, expensive vacations, etc. This wave of spending gave our economy a short-term boost that made it *feel* like everybody was wealthy.

In reality, **the entire housing market was being subsidized by the federal government providing easy money.** The housing bubble had nothing to do with actual supply and demand, and everything to do with the federal government's monetary policy. Seeing an opportunity for "easy" money lured many people who figured they'd get their real estate license and get their piece of the action! And I can't blame them.

During the housing boom, it was hard *not* to be making money in real estate. New listings would sell in days or weeks—not months. It was super easy to get financing. RARELY did a deal collapse because of problems with financing. Banks were giving loans to anyone and everyone. Looking back, this was incredibly stupid, and a major reason why we had a boom and bust cycle in the housing market.

I've heard many people say that becoming a real estate agent is easy. And, again, to be honest, they are probably right. It's really not that hard to take the classes, pass the test, and become an officially licensed Realtor. What is hard, and what separates amateurs from the true professionals, is dedication to the industry. You simply cannot develop expertise or market knowledge by spending ten hours a week.

Think about it this way: Would you feel comfortable having your legal work taken care of by a "part-time attorney?" Or having a major operation done by a "part-time surgeon?" When the proper analogy is made, it seems absurd. I wouldn't want my hair cut by a part-timer much less buying or selling an expensive home!

Now, keep in mind all of these professions require proper licensing. Just like real estate, they do require official "certification." But just because someone is technically licensed doesn't mean you should assume they're an expert! A piece of paper means they were smart enough to pass a test—it's *not* an indicator of true market knowledge, or wisdom that takes *years* to accumulate.

It might sound like I'm bashing part-timers. I'm not! Some of them spent their lives in and around real estate, and now they are semi-retired. Not *all* part time agents are inexperienced or lack market knowledge; however, it's worth repeating the question I posed earlier: would you entrust ***the largest investment you will probably ever make*** to a part-timer who is "dabbling" in real estate?

I mean, really, think about it. . . it's pretty crazy that people would trust a complete amateur to handle the process of buying or selling an asset that will cost *hundreds of thousands* of dollars. When you pay the agent's commission, you are not paying for their time to help you fill out the paperwork at closing. Honestly, if you spent enough time reading the small print, you could probably figure that stuff out by yourself.

The real value provided by an agent is everything that happens up to that point! That is where it is invaluable to have a true expert working on your behalf.

About Adam

After a short stint in the 9-5 world after graduating from college in 2007, Adam Stark entered the Real Estate industry in the fall of 2009 as a single agent for Coldwell Banker in his home town of Jefferson City, MO. (Population 45,000)

With no experience in sales, systems, marketing or business building, Adam ended his first 12 months in Real Estate sales earning just under $13,000 in Net Commission Income. Not one to be discouraged, Adam began investing in himself at a very high level over the next several years – bringing in some of the biggest names in the expert spaces of Real Estate and Internet Marketing to help expedite the journey.

Fast forward to 2016 and Adam now heads a Team of five Agents, two Admin. ISA's and a Transaction Coordinator that closed on over 150 Transactions for the year and $27,000,000 in Total Volume.

Adam has brought a fresh new look in Marketing and Branding to the Industry using Social Media and Direct Response Marketing as his main platforms of Lead Generation. He's authored previous books and has pioneered a new era into the industry. Adam has also shared the stage with some of the best sales and marketing trainers in the world – such as Garrett J. White, Ryan Stewman, Alex Charfen, Jay Kinder, Michael Reese and Hoss Pratt.

His Team goal for 2017 is to sell 200 homes and close on $35,000,000 in Total Sales.

CHAPTER 7

CONFESSIONS OF A TRANSACTIONAL AGENT—

HOW YOU CAN MAKE A FORTUNE, NOT JUST A LIVING

BY RANDY HUNTLEY

The title of this book is called *Real Estate GameChangers.* You'll enjoy chapters that describe extraordinary game-changing accomplishments of agents from across the country in the area of real estate. My fellow co-authors are building high-producing teams, implementing great systems, accounting to various coaches, and basically changing how real estate is transacted.... They are definitely on the cutting edge of technology, leading the way. New agents are teaming up with the experienced ones to learn innovative lead generation techniques. Some agents have even perfected the referral process, while others still focus on old-fashioned door knocking, cold calling, and open houses.

So, what can I possibly add to this book? I've never considered myself a game changer, yet here I am, a featured co-author in *Real Estate GameChangers.* Is there really any game changing left for me to talk about? I say yes, but first the definition of a Game Changer.

Game changer: Someone or something that *completely changes* the way that things are done, thought about, or made.

Let me ask, are you making a living, or making a fortune? There is a difference, you know. Making a living says to me that you are making just enough to pay the bills, cover the mortgage, and perhaps put away a little for college or retirement. Making a fortune means you can take money off the table, you don't have to be consumed with financial worry, you can even leave a legacy to your family or community.

It all comes down to whether you are a transactional agent, or a relational one. Transactional agents certainly do make a living, maybe even a good one; however, relational agents make a fortune!

Two more definitions:

1. **Transactional agent:** one who is friendly, knowledgeable, dependable, honorable, full of integrity, but lives for the next transaction. And after each transaction, a transactional agent disappears and begins from scratch going after the next transaction. Life as a transactional agent is not fun.
2. **Relational agent:** one who is all the above, but does not disappear after the transaction; rather, they continue with and deepen the established relationship, offering assistance and care for years afterward. Life as a relational agent is fun and fulfilling.

The title of my chapter is called "Confessions of a Transactional Agent." Yes, I, Randy Huntley, confess that I am a recovering transactional agent. For nearly 30 years, I've helped my clients buy and/or sell their properties and then simply moved on to the next one, seeming to forget them and the fact that we had the beginnings of a great relationship. I didn't mean to do it, it just happened. Time went on and rather than take time to check in on my clients, I thought it was more important to look for the next transaction. This happens quite a bit in real estate because after all, if you don't sell, you don't get paid. For years I spent most of my available hours hunting down the next transaction – and I made a living, you know, enough to pay my bills, cover my mortgage and save for college and retirement.

How about the agents who considered themselves 'relational'? Well, besides continuing their established relationship many of these agents are well on their way to making a fortune! What??!!! Yes, they simply extended their care past the settlement and had no real timeline. They just related and cared.

Is this the game changer? Simply relating to clients well after the settlement IS the game changer. In the next couple of paragraphs I hope to teach you what not to do. Believe me there are thousands of books teaching us what to do, including techniques of relating to clients after the sale; however, I am going to quantify my transactional experience in real dollars with the hope of driving home the point that transactional agents are heading for a dead end, while relational agents are soaring to exponential income.

Say, what would happen if you and your significant other went 7-10 days without even talking, no communication whatsoever? What do you suppose each is thinking? The relationship begins to break down, anger sets in, misunderstandings develop, and everything you worked toward is crumbling to the point that one of you is eventually going to move on.

Oddly enough, this is exactly what happens when transactional agents settle and move on in search of the next one. All the goodwill, great feelings, warm regards deteriorate, and clients move on – possibly to other agents years later. Remember that homeowners tend to buy and sell every 5 to 7 years. Transactional agents don't respect this, but relational agents do.

Just how easy is it to just continue the established relationship? For relational agents it comes naturally, but not for transactional ones. I think all agents know that its their job to stay front of mind so that we naturally become trusted sources for their real estate-related questions. In fact, they come to depend on us so much that they will continue to ask us for referrals to plumbers, roofers, electricians, and many other house-related trades. Relational agents get to know their clients much better AFTER the sale than during the sale. Transactional agents re-invent themselves and begin looking for the next client.

Now for my own game changer:

Recently after being prodded by my real estate assistant for several months, I decided to re-constitute my Christmas card list. As I was assembling names, I actually forgot who some of them were, even though they were some of my past clients! Of course I lost track of hundreds of phone numbers, email addresses, birthdays, anniversaries, family members, and whatever other critical information I collected along the way. However, when I wanted to confirm an address or two, I turned to the MLS to research tax records. Easy. Just confirm the address, add it to my 'new', re-constituted database, label my Christmas cards and my annual chore would have been done.

Well, except for one slight problem, the tax record indicated that the house was sold last June. What??!! They didn't tell me they wanted to sell! I WAS THEIR AGENT! I SOLD THEM THAT HOUSE! WHY WOULD THEY WANT SOMEONE ELSE?? That's not all. Curiosity caused me to cross reference their name and what do you know, they were safely tucked into another house twice as expensive as the one they just sold. The average commission in my market area is $12,000 to $15,000, with gusts up to $30K, so I quickly did the math and then felt really sick. At this point I was stunned and hurt wondering why my friends, my clients, forsook me. Self-doubt overtook me and I had no clue why they did what they did, but one thing for sure, I was offended.

After a few days of recovery, because time has a way of healing,

I got after the Christmas card list again. Privately, I forgave 'my' clients for their transgression! Looking through my list I needed to check another address and instantly felt sick again. Groundhog Day. The same thing happened. This time my personal friends, not just clients, listed with another agent and purchased with the same one. Why is this happening to me?

Well, as the chapter title indicates, I now have to confess that between 2015 and 2016, after a thorough screening of my entire database (Christmas card list), I missed out on thirteen transactions equaling approximately $234,000 GCI. As a final kicker, I found out about #13 because my Christmas card was returned. Go figure.

This was a dagger to my heart and it took several hours of searching my own soul trying to figure why I kept hemorrhaging transactions. I finally admitted that I was the cause. Of course, I was present at settlement because most agents are. However, relational agents begin after-sale systems of care and contact, and community transactional agents like myself figure that the clients are ours for life and therefore we convince ourselves of that. It means that transactional agents *take for granted* that the client loyalty will never erode, while relational agents guarantee it.

Okay, we're at the point in this chapter where you're thinking, how did I ever make a living selling real estate? What, with being transactional and all. . . Well, I wasn't always transactional, in fact, I was quite relational in how I operated my business. I called into my database regularly, wrote about 30-50 personal notes a month, popped by friend's and client's houses just because. Ah yes, real estate life was good. . . until life started getting in the way. Of course I had a family to attend to, church obligations, reserve military duty, vacations to consider, existing clients to serve, classes to teach, students to mentor, emergencies to respond to, and the list of distractions became endless! My problem was that I didn't know a lot about prioritizing and strategic thinking, and I just let everything get in the way of relationships. That's it. When relationships begin to crumble, transactional selling takes over. After all, I still had to sell to make a living to pay the bills, cover the mortgage, and put a little away for college and retirement. I got to the point where making a fortune was just an unfulfilled dream.

Enter our productivity coach, Ben Jones. Ha! Timing is everything – Ben walks into my office at the exact moment I confirmed #13 from the paragraph above sold the house I sold them, and bought a house almost twice as expensive from the other agent! You can imagine what my response was when he asked me how it was going! Ben let me vent for ten minutes before he even took a breath to speak. I was spewing a double-barrel-sized amount of blame, whining, complaining, and pitiful. And then he told me to get relational. Make those calls and write those notes, and stop by your friend's house to say hello. No need to ask about real estate related subjects. Just show them that you care and real estate relating will once again become fun and fulfilling for me. And profitable.

Here's the Game Changer: Take care of your client database and guard it like it's worth a million dollars. Care for your friends and clients and communicate with them regularly. They will be loyal to you as long as you are loyal to them. Don't go more than a few weeks without offering some kind of communication like a call, or perhaps a handwritten personal note. Dropping by the house occasionally reinforces your relationship. Make time for your Christmas card list. Don't be afraid to reach out to check in and share stories of friendship. Offer neighborhood market information or similar items of value. Never assume you are always going to be their agent – it will keep you sharp and tuned in to your database and their real estate-related plans. Finally, get a coach or at least an accountability partner to help you keep on track.

I wish I could have produced a hugely dramatic and profound game-changing chapter. Instead, I hope I was able to convince a transactional agent or two that making a living is okay, but why not strive to make a fortune by being relational?

About Randy

Randy Huntley has been a Northern Virginia Realtor for nearly 30 years and also owns Property Management Advisors, LLC. He has continued to provide first-class service to his buyer and seller clients, as well as landlords worldwide. Currently he is a multi-million-dollar producing Associate Broker representing Keller Williams Metro Center, Tysons Corner, VA. Randy enjoys teaching real estate principles along with coaching and mentoring rookie agents into their first year of service.

Originally from Iowa, Randy is a recently retired 30-year veteran of the U.S. Marine Corps and U.S. Army. Randy and his wife, Sue, have been married for 38 years, have four children, and eight (soon to be ten) grandchildren. The Huntley's are fortunate that all their children and grandchildren live in the Northern Va. region!

Randy concentrates his business in Northern Va. and is also licensed in the District of Columbia. Selling real estate and managing residential property are his true passions because as he says, "We're in the 'Peace of Mind' Business. I receive a significant sense of satisfaction knowing that my clients put their faith in me as their agent and property manager. In other words, my clients know that I've got their backs!"

Randy employs a staff of competent, caring, and very enthusiastic professionals – all ready to serve their clients. Randy's processing staff does not leave anything to guess work, and his property management team is always ready to handle everything from very small problems to catastrophic occurrences.

The positive feedback his team receives encourages them to strive for constant improvement and efficiency.

- "Thanks for all you do for us!" July L., Arl, VA.
- "We just love working with your team! It makes my husband and I feel like we are your best, most valued clients!" Elaine W., Yakima, WA.

Randy credits many mentors such as Brian Buffini, Michael Reese, Jay Kinder, Steve Gaskins, Gary Keller, and Dave Ramsey for setting wonderful examples of success in business. But Randy credits one leader and friend most of all for re-directing him into relational selling instead of transactional selling: Thank you Benjamin Jones, Productivity Coach of KW Metro Center, for listening and offering keen insight that caused Randy's Game Changing attitude to soar in 2017!

CHAPTER 8

HUMANITY IN A DIGITAL WORLD:

YES, IT IS POSSIBLE!

BY THOMAS ECHEA and LISA ECHEA

The digital world is an incredible place. It gives us access to data, resources, and visually-appealing information instantaneously. It has changed our world in a substantial way. Some debate if this is good or bad, but its existence cannot be disputed. For most types of business, how we conduct it will never be the same again. Despite this, there is one thing that the digital world can never replace—and this is the human touch that is so vital to some business's success and livelihood. Real estate is one of these businesses.

When it comes to sales and serving clients' best interests, talking about the personal touch is nothing new. It's a conversation that's been had in just about every office that works in sales in some way. But did you know…you can still get back to basics? Before social media took over the conversation, people-to-people connections were the cornerstone of business. This is still true. People always have and always will love the personalized people touch. Including the 86% of people who begin their real estate search online.

Imagine… You have a business where you create connections with the 14% that seek out the human connection to begin their process, while also having a way to connect with the 86% that begin the process in the digital world. This is what our team has done and the impact is not only personally rewarding, but also proving itself to be the ideal formula—a human touch in the virtual world!

In today's real estate industry, far too many customers feel agents are only in the business for the commission. If you want to be ultra-successful, your customers must intuitively know you have their best interest in mind. These win-win working relationships embody good real estate business.
~ Jeff Lippman, Broker/Owner RE/MAX House of Real Estate

People like it when you give them your time and energy, treating them like a friend the first time you meet them. The human touch is everything, in both our personal lives and our business life. We are all in business to succeed and it's no secret that we need to earn a living at what we do. For Realtors®, this is our commission. Still, it cannot be the driving force of our actions. Focusing on money first is likely to lead to one thing—dwelling on the monies you have not been able to earn. Create a connection first, and then the rest will fall into place. We've both operated other successful businesses for nearly twenty-five years before entering into the real estate industry. The same was true in those businesses, as well. It's a universal business principle.

By helping people achieve their happiness or have their needs fulfilled, your rewards will come. Nothing makes for a better experience than a customer knowing they are working with a professional who doesn't just say they have their best interests in mind, they emphasize this truth through their actions and rapport. Plus, it's fun. There's no more invigorating way to cultivate business. Less burn-out. Better transactions. More joy.

FIVE PILLARS FOR BUILDING A BUSINESS WITH HUMANITY

The way we communicate with others and with ourselves ultimately determines the quality of our lives.
~ Anthony Robbins

The pillars that it takes to keep 'the humanity' in business are solid. They are the hallmark of businesses that standout amongst their competition. Additionally, they show the distinct line that exists between excuses and execution.

Pillar #1: The Personal Touch

A common thought process for many agents is to feel the personal touch criterion is met by making one phone call to a potential lead. It is more involved than this. You need to listen to all the needs people have and learn about them as individuals. Go above and beyond. An example may be finding out that a potential lead really loves to golf. Send them an article about an upcoming tournament in the area. Always remember, it isn't a race to get off the phone. Take as much time as is necessary to genuinely engage and build trust.

Have a conversation, not an inquisition.

The art of conversation comes naturally to some, and is learned by others. Dale Carnegie said, "You can make more friends in two months by becoming interested in other people than you can in two years by trying to get other people interested in you." This takes practice and sincerity, but it can be done. It's worth the effort because it makes the follow-up phone call more personal and powerful. These things are remembered because of their genuine nature.

Pillar #2: Build a People First Business

One technology we love is our lead generation site. It's effective, and gives us access to potential clients. When that lead comes in, the people first part of our business begins. One of our team members makes a call so we can establish rapport with the leads via a conversation and through answering their questions. There are always questions! If you are not well versed in the art of conversation, don't worry! We've been doing this long enough that it's easy for our team, but with a combination of base scripts to build from and knowing your business thoroughly help you master good conversations. Operate at an elite level.

After this, we make sure this potential client is put in the right hands so we can ensure they get what they are looking for. Additionally, we do something that has proven itself to be pivotal in developing the human connection—we send a video email. These emails are great for a variety of reasons, including:

- Many of our leads are from out of town. Creating the people first aspect of our business and allowing for a relationship to grow despite not being face-to-face suddenly becomes possible.
- We can recap what we have discussed via telephone, which shows that we were vested listeners. Additionally, we are building a relationship, which is the start of something with numerous benefits down the line, not the least of which is career satisfaction and happiness.
- Based on the art of conversation which takes place in the initial telephone call, we have something of meaning to add in the video email. It's unique and personalized, which is an essential part of building a people-first business.

The only thing you need to be mindful of is that timing is everything. It does have to be quick, or this potential lead will be on to the next thing. If you are not calling, someone else is! The initial call allows you to show them how you are going to engage them with value-driven content over the next week. This layout of communication shows you are serious, you care, and that you are dedicated. With our strategy, our team has five touches within one week of the initial inquiry.

Pillar #3: Value Personal Interaction above All

Personal interaction offers a great many things, but one of the most valuable is the opportunity to engage so you can evaluate how serious the person at the other end of the line is. Are they ready to buy or sell immediately? Or, are they putting out their feelers for some time in the future (anywhere from three months to a year out)? All options are okay; they just determine your approach to your personal interaction.

Give back to people what you would like to receive as an individual.

You have to know when people will be set to "go" on a transaction. If their "go" is in the future, we put them on a nurturing campaign, which has proven to be quite effective for us. With this, we find ways to reach out to these people on a monthly basis, via video emails or follow-up calls. This has resulted in us converting a large percentage of future prospects.

Pillar #4: Always Show Humility, Honesty, and Respect

Being honest, transparent, and helpful to clients' means that you must be forthright. If you don't have an answer, tell them "I don't have the answer, but I will get it for you." Don't just give opinions or statements that have prefaces similar to "if I were you" or "in my opinion."

Another helpful thing to do is not be afraid to be relatable. Purchasing a home is one of the biggest transactions in many people's lives, which can create nervousness. Show people you get this and you are a true professional who will guide them throughout their real estate transaction.

Pillar #5: Focus Time and Energy on Each Client

People want to work with other people. Sure, they'll use the internet to get some basic information, but if you want to buy or sell a home you cannot avoid working with people. Be the person they want to work with! No amount of looking at images online, taking 3D virtual tours, and doing preliminary research can replace the role of a Realtor® at some point. This is why you need to:

- Build trust
- Make it tangible
- Guide people to their goal with a genuine interest

You can be loyal to clients, and by approaching your business the right way, they'll be loyal to you, too. We even have a "loyalty agreement" that we sign with our clients. It's not legally binding, but it's a sign of respect to each other. We're in this together and understand each other's intentions and expectations, and respect each other's time invested.

VIDEO EMAILS: A RESULTS-DRIVEN HUMAN TOUCH

Video emails are one thing that have helped to revolutionize the humanity of business in a digital world.

We mentioned the video emails already, but they are worthy of a quick note as to why they have proven so important for us. Regardless of what your business is, you are likely to find value in video emails for growing it and connecting with clients. We don't own a video email service, but we certainly are advocates of them. Why? Because they are so effective!

Our experiences with video emails have been going strong for about three years now. We have had more sales as a result, earned more referrals, built better rapport, and given a value-added touch to our transactions that resonates on a personal level.

A majority of our clients are from out of town looking for their second homes and/or investment properties here in the Tri-County area – which consists of Palm Beach, Fort Lauderdale and Miami (all of which we serve). Many times we don't meet them face-to-face until their closing, if even then. They get to know us through video emails and FaceTime or Skype tours we give them of properties they are interested in. These transactions run as smoothly as if they were right next to us because of these human touches. We've built a friendship and a level of trust that is necessary for success.

These experiences are so great and rewarding; a way to not let the communication and connectedness dissipate in a digital transaction. The power that video brings technology-wise is amazing, but it also is a stark reminder of the power of the basics of communication. There truly is no reason to sacrifice technology for human connectedness or human connectedness for technology. Don't buy into that notion that you can't make a great new world that incorporates the best of these two things.

USING TECHNOLOGY TO WORK WITH PEOPLE

Use technology as a tool that allows you to serve people better.

There are so many great rewards that come from focusing on humanity first in everything you do, business or personal. For us, we've noticed that this has allowed us to be more present in our every interaction. By not being distracted, you become engaged. When this happens everything falls into place. You work better with your team. You get to know your clients better, and in a more authentic manner. And you learn how to use technology and digital communications in a manner which shows your genuine nature, that you were listening, which builds rapport.

Being "too busy" for this really isn't acceptable. We are all on the same twenty-four hour clock and have only so many hours in a day to get everything done. It's one of the links that bonds us as people who want to achieve things. It's only through leveraging our humanity that we can have the awareness to really value how important this is. At the end of the day that is really what matters—the value of the human touch and person-to-person interaction. It's the heart of serving others.

About Thomas and Lisa

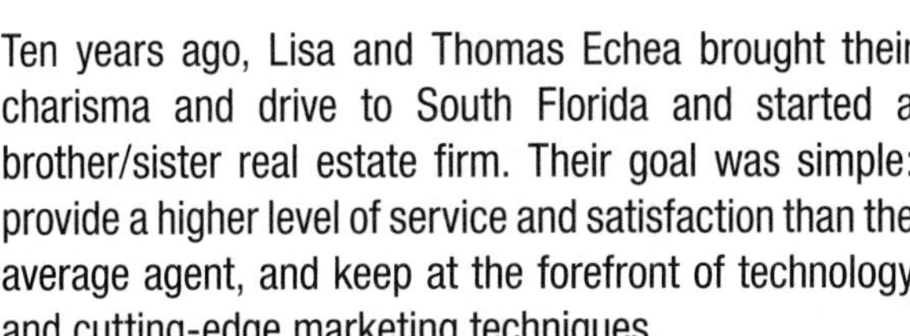

Ten years ago, Lisa and Thomas Echea brought their charisma and drive to South Florida and started a brother/sister real estate firm. Their goal was simple: provide a higher level of service and satisfaction than the average agent, and keep at the forefront of technology and cutting-edge marketing techniques.

For many people, buying or selling their own home is a daunting and scary process. Although many consumers start online, often times the sheer amount of information can be overwhelming. The unknowns of buying a home shouldn't keep clients from obtaining their dream home. The key to staying a step ahead of the stress and pressure is having an experienced and knowledgeable real estate agent on your side. With over 1000 people moving to Florida every day, buyers and sellers should not settle for just any cookie-cutter real estate agent. When prospects work with the Echea Group, they are working with a real estate team with a proven track record of success for their clients.

Whether you're a first-time buyer or a seasoned investor, Lisa will walk you through step by step, making sure the process is as effortless as possible. Armed with excellent negotiation skills and acute business sense in every transaction, Lisa Echea becomes a close ally to the buyer or seller.

Raising her family in Plantation, Florida (with her husband and two boys), Lisa is an expert in the surrounding neighborhoods, and has a wealth of knowledge pertaining to top schools, restaurants and shopping districts. The proof of this is in the many five-star Zillow reviews she has received from her clients.

To describe Thomas as 'personal' and 'passionate' would sum him up perfectly. What separates him from the many others in his field of expertise is the way he communicates with not only his clients, but everyone around him. An answer for his success is simple; he embraces and harnesses new technologies while keeping himself grounded with that personal touch and a dash of charm.

Thomas puts technology to work for you. His internet presence includes dozens of state-of-the-art websites and social media outlets, all designed to generate maximum exposure for client's listings, and lead to higher offers and quicker sales.

The Echea Group's strategies and performance have quickly pushed them to become a top-producing team under RE/MAX House of Real Estate. Both Lisa and Thomas have earned their CHSA and CHBA designation as well as the coveted Certified Luxury Home Marketing Specialist (CLHMS) designations. The Echea Group averages a sale every three days, bringing an eye for detail that few can rival. You'll be hard-pressed to find another real estate team more in-touch with the South Florida real estate market than Lisa and Thomas Echea.

CHAPTER 9

MARKETING IS KEY

BY SHELLY SALAS

I don't have enough fingers to count the amount of times I've been contacted by a seller who hired a discounted realtor and they did nothing but put a sign in the yard. When they call me, they are frustrated that their home hasn't sold. I recall a particular client of mine (we'll call her Sarah) who called me as soon as her listing agreement was over with her real estate agent. She lived outside our area, so her home was sitting vacant for over 6 months! Listening to her frustration, she was now contemplating on whether it even made sense for her to continue to try to sell. Sarah was willing to let her home go into foreclosure because she now had two mortgages. She stressed to me that she really cared about her credit and that's why she reached out to me, but that if I couldn't sell it, she was going to let the bank take it back.

It's stories like this that really have me question what are sellers thinking when they interview a real estate agent. What I have found throughout the years is that some sellers will select a real estate agent simply because they discounted their commission and they thought they would end up with more money in their pocket. Each day that passes by (and the home doesn't sell) the homeowner is paying daily interest on the loan, utilities remain on, lawn has to be maintained, etc. The reality is that it will cost them more in the end. The discount real estate agent is no longer a discount.

When hiring a discounted real estate agent, they can't provide the marketing exposure that a seller needs in order to sell their home. There is so much competition in today's market that if you want your home to sell, you have to make sure it reaches as much of an audience as possible. Your average real estate agent will simply put a sign in the yard and place the home in the local multiple listing service (MLS) and then they hope and pray that it will sell. But the probability of the buyer driving by and calling the For Sale sign and buying that particular home is low. That is a big prayer they are asking for on the seller's mortgage dime.

In Sarah's case, I obviously didn't want her to go into foreclosure, but I understood her frustration and desperation. I told her to allow me to go look at her home so I could see the condition of the property and properly evaluate it. I wanted to see if she was overpriced or if it was simply a marketing exposure issue. After evaluating the home, it was, as I suspected, a marketing issue. I told Sarah that her home was priced well and that if I listed her home, it would sell. I sold several homes in her neighborhood, I knew it very well. I asked her to trust in me and my marketing, I was confident that I would be able to sell her home.

Sure enough, after placing her home on the market we had an offer in just 15 days! The marketing exposure that I provided was well beyond what her previous realtor provided. Sarah was ecstatic and beyond grateful that she had an offer. I knew her financial burden was starting to consume her and I really wanted to help her. I could tell from her voice that her stress level was now going down. I was so happy for her.

Sarah's issue is one that is too common, and yet, every time a seller calls me and shares their story with me, I just shake my head in disbelief (if they're across from me, I secretly do it in my head, lol). I shake my head because I can't believe that in today's market, a seller will choose a discount for marketing exposure. Don't get me wrong, I too love a discount, I always ask the employee at a store or restaurant if they offer a military discount.

But when it comes to such a huge investment like your home, you can't go with the person that offers you a discounted commission. As the good saying goes, "You get what you pay for."

Clearly, real estate agents do fundamentally the same things in the broad general sense; they list and sell homes for sellers, they help buyers find a home and help them buy it. This is like saying all doctors and hospitals do essentially the same things. However, as we know, this is not true. There are those heart surgeons, for example, that are so good at what they do, that people will travel across the nation to have them perform the surgery. On the other hand, there are other doctors who struggle to fill their waiting rooms. There are hospitals that people won't go to because "Oh, it's that one!" vs. the hospitals that people will travel to the next town to seek, because they are that good.

If someone has a medical need, they will look for the best doctor out there, they don't want just any doctor. So, for the very significant financial matter of selling their home, a seller should look for the most experienced, most successful real estate agent they can find in their area. If this describes you, then now you are starting to realize that there's no way ALL real estate agents are the same.

When I tell you that marketing is key, it really is. I see homes on the market all the time that a realtor has placed in our multiple listing service (MLS) and it looks like they literally took the pictures of the home with their cell phone. This is such a disservice to their client and again I just shake my head. They most likely are always discounting their commission so that they can't even afford to buy a great camera to take amazing photos of their listing. It's like there's no pride in their work. To me, we have that one opportunity to retain the buyer as they are looking at hundreds of homes. I want them to pick my listing, so I have to make sure it looks amazing.

Sellers should have high expectations of their real estate agent.

They should do an autopsy on their listing. Look it up online and see what the consumer is viewing. Read the description, does it properly describe the home. There's another soap box I can get into, but won't. Ok, ok, I can't help myself but I promise I will make it brief. Along with bad photos, if you only knew how many times I read over a marketing description that a real estate agent wrote on a home they have listed and it has 1 to 2 sentences, or better yet, no description! I always think to myself, how can the seller be ok with this?

I believe sellers don't know what to expect, so they are blindly trusting the real estate agent that they hired to sell their home. The problem is that most real estate agents don't know what to do when it comes to marketing. Or perhaps they can't financially afford to spend a lot of money on marketing because they are not that successful or have given up part of their commission to get the listing. And now it doesn't make financial sense to spend marketing dollars. Whatever the reason, at the end of the day, it's the seller who carries the financial burden each day the home sits on the market.

It's important that sellers do a little research on the real estate agent they are hiring. What is their success rate? What is their marketing strategy? Read their reviews. This is a large financial transaction, you want to put it in the proper hands, not the cheapest hands.

A recent client of mine (we'll call him Tom), called me after his home was on the market with another real estate agent and his home didn't sell. He told me his frustrating story as well (it was similar to Sarah's), but I remember him particularly because he mentioned that his wife had found me online and wanted to hire me to sell their home, but he vetoed her vote because someone at work had a friend that was a real estate agent. He went with them instead. After months of no activity, he fired the real estate agent and called me. He said and I quote: "I should've listened to my wife and gone with you in the first place." We placed his home on the market and it went under contract very quickly and they too were happy. They were able to move to their new duty station without having to worry about having a vacant home left behind.

Had Tom researched his co-worker's referral of the real estate agent, he would have known about their success rate and would have been able to see what they were doing with the current homes they had listed. He would have definitely saved himself some headaches, I'm sure.

When I meet with a client, I will always explain to them what to expect throughout the process of selling their home. There's a lot that happens behind the scenes and if you're not in our field you probably don't know. I feel that it's my duty to inform my clients of the process. I want them to have high expectations of me. This keeps my feet to the fire because I don't want to under deliver on their expectations of me. This is how sellers should be with ALL real estate agents. Hold their feet to the fire. This is our profession, we should be experts at it, or do what it takes to become the expert. But nevertheless, if they are hired by a seller to sell their home, they should provide the best-of-the-best service possible.

Here's a quick outline that will help you stay on the right path when hiring a real estate agent to sell your home. It's very simple, I've broken it down to six easy steps:

Step 1—Research top real estate agents in your area.

Step 2—Look over their success rate.

Step 3—Read their reviews.

Step 4—Look over the current homes they have listed.

A. How do the pictures look?
B. Does the marketing description make you want to buy it?

Step 5—When meeting with the real estate agent, ask them what do they do for marketing.

Remember marketing is Key!

Step 6—Whatever you do, don't be tempted to hire someone because they are discounted.

Remember, you get what you pay for!

I've sold hundreds of homes in my area. I love what I do, I love my career. My career has allowed me to meet lots of amazing people. I have so many stories I would love to be able to write about but there are not enough pages here to write on. However, if there is something that most of my clients that come to me (after their home has not sold with someone else) have in common, it's that they regret not doing the research from the beginning.

Most of us do research on smaller things like shoes, furniture, cars, etc. But when it comes to a transaction dealing with such a large, financial decision, I just shake my head when sellers hire someone because they were "nice." "Nice" doesn't sell your home but marketing sure does!

Don't forget the six simple steps I outlined for you and select the "best-of-the-best!"

About Shelly

I love real estate. I got my real estate license back in 2005 assisting my husband Luis. I was a full-time college student at the time but I wanted to help my husband. As time went by and I started meeting our clients, I found a love for this field. I switched my degree and the rest as they say, is history.

I am a first-generation child of migrant parents. My parents instilled in me the need to work hard and always reach for my goals. My dad told me at a very young age "Mija, if you don't want to be a migrant worker like me, get your education and do whatever you want to do in life." Those words have always stuck with me. It's these words that build my fundamental desire and determination to do something I truly enjoyed in life.

I decided to join the Army when I was 19 years old. I loved my time in the military. Being able to serve our country is something that I am very proud of. I was the first one in my family to join the military. It was scary for my parents when I told them. However, it was the best decision I ever made. But now I can proudly say that I am an Army Veteran.

I am a proud mother of three amazing kids. I have an amazing and supportive husband whom I love dearly. They are my world. It takes special people to be able to handle a real estate agent's crazy and hectic schedule, and they are truly the best family I could've ever dreamed of.

I graduated from the University of Mary Hardin Baylor (Go Crusaders!). It was tough going to school full-time with small children, a husband and trying to work, but again, my dad's words were always in the back of my head. I was determined to graduate. When I did, I became the first person in my family to do so. It was such a great milestone to reach.

Throughout my career, I have received distinguished awards for my overall real estate success. I have been featured in *The Wall Street Journal* several years for being in the top 250 agents/teams nationwide. I have also received several top corporate awards for my successful real estate transactions from my corporate clients.

I've sold over a thousand homes throughout my career and every time a client buys a home I get the same happy feeling for them that I did when I first started. I love being able to help my seller clients sell their existing home to then move on to their next venture. I love real estate and am so grateful for all the people I have met, helped and developed a relationship with – during my career.

You can contact Shelly at:

- 254-616-0356

Or visit her website:

- shellysalas.com

CHAPTER 10

PUT MORE MONEY IN YOUR POCKET WHEN YOU SELL

BY TJ VITENSE

REAL ESTATE AGENT COSTS SELLER $20,000!

An interesting message flashes across my phone. My close friend is texting me to tell me about his friend who just sold a home in one day…for $10,000 over asking price…with multiple offers. My phone proceeds to ring within minutes of receiving the text…

"Hey, I can't believe how fast my friend sold his home, and for $10,000 over asking price! He was asking $200,000 and sold for $210,000."—I hear on the other end of the phone. I try to explain to my friend what is currently going on in the market and explain that his friend's situation isn't abnormal in today's market. As I probe a little deeper into the property that just sold (as I'm always curious what other professionals/advisors do to net their clients the most money), an alarm slowly starts going off in the pit of my stomach.

By the time he finishes telling me about the property, a full-blown, gut-wrenching, stomach-turning sickness has fully kicked in. Just when I think it can't get any worse, he ends with, "The agent who helped my friend only charged $2,500 to sell it! How can he be so cheap?"

Within minutes, I send my friend info on three, recent home sales in the same area for prices ranging from $225,000 to $260,000. I explain to him that there is no reason the home shouldn't have been originally listed for at least $230,000, or more, based on everything he had told me.

Have you ever felt sick to your stomach because you know something just wasn't right? I couldn't get this out of my head for weeks! It is a Realtor's job and moral obligation to put our client's interests ahead of anyone else's throughout the entire home-sale transaction. And while I believe you get what you pay for, the story I had been told just didn't sit right with me… (and still doesn't to this day).

DEATH OF THE REAL ESTATE AGENT

With more and more real estate agents running around in today's market place, it is imperative that you realize, as a consumer, you have a difficult choice to make. But, more importantly, that you have a voice to be heard! Stop putting up with the average real estate agent! I don't care if it's your cousin, brother/sister-in-law, or, heck, I don't care if it's your mom! The average real estate agent in today's market doesn't possess the skills needed to guide you through today's complex real estate transactions, let alone know the market well enough to help you put the most money in your pocket! You need a trusted Advisor – an expert in the field who can put you and your family in the best position possible when the time comes to buy or sell your home.

Want to know why you don't want the average, frustrated, real estate agent and need a true Advisor on your side?

1. **The average agent sells less than eight homes per year:**

   Really… eight homes!! Either that agent is part-time or has no clue what is going on in the market. An agent who sells eight homes per year is not putting enough food on the table for his/her family and definitely doesn't have money left over to pay bills. This isn't even taking into consideration the dues/fees that realtors require to be an agent…it's not cheap to be a Real Estate Agent! If your agent is selling eight homes, or less, per year, do they really have the skills necessary to put you in the best position possible? Or, better yet, will they give you the right advice, knowing they need your home to sell in order to put food on their table? I always in my heart hope they do, but, unfortunately, that isn't always the case.

2. **It only takes, nationally, an average of 90 hours to obtain your real estate license:**

   Are you kidding me?!?! Only 90 hours, and you think someone has the skills necessary to know the market and help put you and your family in the best position possible when it comes time to buy or sell? It's funny that you can be a Real Estate Agent with only 90 hours of training, but it takes a Cosmetologist 1,500+ hours of training to be certified to cut hair! I don't know about you, but my home is a little bit more important to me than my hair. Now, I'm a guy, so ladies, maybe that's different for you. But really, think about that…with only 90 hours of training, someone is expected to have all the knowledge to help you with the largest purchase or sale you will ever make!! You need a trusted Expert, a true Advisor on your side to help you make the decisions that can determine if you lose or make tens-of-thousands of dollars. I don't know about you, but I'd prefer to put more money in my pocket at the end of the day. That, my friend, is what a trusted Advisor and true Expert in the market place can do for you!

3. **Only 45% of real estate agents spend less than $500 per year on training & development:**

   Again, it is our job to help you with your largest investment. At a minimum, we should be going to, at least, one conference per year to focus on and improve our skills. Whether that is marketing, negotiating, psychology, or professional sales training, there are always things to learn. True professionals are constantly growing and improving in order to provide their clients with the best tools and service possible.

ADVISOR REWRITES THE SCRIPT ON THE PROCESS YOU MUST FOLLOW TO SELL FOR TOP DOLLAR

No two homes are exactly the same, no two agents are the same, and no two marketing plans are the same. . . but, before you ever get to the point of selling your home, you must, I mean, absolutely MUST sit down and come up with a plan, if you truly want to sell your home for top dollar.

First, you must understand there are things you can proactively do on the front end of listing your home for sale to net the most amount of money. The number one most important thing is to sit down with a true Expert Advisor, someone who can completely understand your situation. Why, you might ask. . .

Any home that is for sale in any market place will always sell for a high or a low in the market place. You need to understand, at a minimum, these four things in order to influence your home's potential buyer and attract the highest offer possible:

How to Create an Unforgettable Listing That Attracts Top Dollar

1. The average agent will use a CMA (Comparative/Competitive Market Analysis). The CMA has been used since the beginning of time with real estate agents, and it's an antiquated way to value a property. It's like driving down the highway using your rearview mirror to look into the future and where we are going, right now. An Expert Advisor will take into account outside threats; things like the current interest rate trends, local absorption rates, new construction starts, and local market conditions. You'll also need to review the local supply and demand trends in your

area to truly understand how to position your home in the market place to attract top dollar when you sell.

2. Your home has to stand out from the crowd. Even in a market with low inventory, you always have some competition. If you study any market, money moves to differentiation. Think of it this way. . . Imagine you're selling your car, and so is your neighbor, and so is the local car dealer across the street. Who sells for more? (circle one):

   a. Your neighbor – he doesn't clean his car, and it has junk and wrappers laying around, along with a flat tire.
   b. You – it's cleaned, it's been washed and waxed, and it looks nice and presentable.
   c. The dealer – it's washed, waxed and has that fresh, new car smell, plus it's a certified pre-owned vehicle.

   All things considered, the certified, pre-owned vehicle (the one with the most to offer) attracts a higher offer. Similarly, you can position your home the same way in the market place.

   For example, did you know a home that has been properly staged (by a professional) can attract an offer of 6 to 10% more than a home that has not been staged? Plus, the staged home sells two times faster than the non-staged homes. This is just one example of the many steps necessary to position your home in the market place for top dollar.

3. You must understand how to EXPOSE your home to the largest audience possible. Your real estate agent should be able to show you how he/she is allocating marketing dollars to bring in the largest audience of prospective buyers.

   Let me explain, as you must understand where buyers are coming from. Did they find information from the internet, an open house, a yard sign, direct mailing, etc.? You must have a strategy to attract people from each of these potential sources so you can maximize your chances of finding a buyer.

For example, currently 92% of buyers are using the internet. This is important to understand because then we can specifically target where buyers are looking and where they are coming from. So, if we know which top websites buyers use when looking for a home, then we can allocate a portion of the marketing budget towards those specific sites, so we can be sure your home is in front of the most eyeballs possible.

But, there is more to understand than just getting your home in front of people online. You must also understand that in addition to your home showing up online, it's also important that it is presented well. You need professional photos, you need to be able to track how many people have viewed the home, where they viewed the home, and how to use copywriting to get potential buyers to take action to come and see your home.

It comes down to supply and demand, and if we make your home stand out from the crowd and create enough demand, then we can ideally attract higher than market value offers. Unfortunately, the typical frustrated real estate agent only puts a sign in the yard, places it on the MLS and prays it sells in time to pay his/her bills.

4. You must understand that 88% of potential buyers for your home will work with a Real Estate agent. Aside from marketing to the potential buyer pool, you must 100% market to the local real estate professionals. They have 88% of the buyers, yet they are often the number one source overlooked when it comes time to allocate marketing dollars to attracting buyers and top dollar.

The tricky part with this is understanding that, more than likely, we will deal with the average agent who sells less than a handful of homes per year. Well, there are ways to position the home and incentivize the agent who brings the buyer to attract top dollar. As I said before, just keep in the back of your mind the fact that the average agent barely sells enough to put food on the table, yet the buyer is looking to the agent for advice and guidance on what to offer YOU for your home. There are a few stealth strategies you can use to get the agent excited to sell your home, and that, my friend, is something we share during our seller consultations. So if you'd like to find out how to do this, we are just a phone call away.

"TRADITIONAL" REAL ESTATE AGENTS HAVE FAILED YOU!

The traditional real estate agent model is broken; it's flawed. . . there is no denying this fact. Real Estate Brokerages across the country are looking to fill empty seats in their offices, everyday. It's not about the consumer, it's about how many agents the Brokerage can acquire for the company to do a "deal" or two, and then move on to the next homebuyer or seller. Keep in mind, these same untrained and unprofessional agents are running around with 90 hours of experience to play with your family's largest investment.

You can no longer rely on the biggest company, your buddy or friend, the agent with the most signs, or the agent who has been in the business 30 years and has fallen behind the times. The real estate industry needs a shake up and ***the standards in this industry must and will be raised*** by true professionals, Expert Advisors, who can walk you through the process and truly help you position your home in the market place to attract top dollar, and put the most amount of money in your pocket at the end of the day.

An entire book could be dedicated and written on the subject of what it takes to market your home for sale and position it so it sells for the most money. Many have tried. When you're ready to buy or sell your next home, make sure you reach out to a local Expert Advisor. You can't afford to risk your family's largest investment with an amateur.

HELP ME GIVE THE REAL ESTATE INDUSTRY A FACELIFT

While months have passed since my friend's buddy sold his home for $20,000 less than he should have, it makes me no less sick to my stomach to think about it. I know, in my heart of hearts, that the home seller in this situation wasn't told what he really needed to hear. The agent that listed his home should be ashamed of the advice he gave, all for the sake of making a quick sale.

Being a realtor is one of the greatest professions in the world, in my opinion, and it's our duty, job, and moral obligation to help you, the consumer, make the best decision possible. Help me shake this industry up! Use your voice and let the market see you are no longer 'ok' with that status quo, contact an Expert in your local market place, and if you can't find one, please look me up and I'll get you in touch with one, today!

About TJ

TJ Vitense was born and raised in the Madison, WI, area and fell in love with real estate at a young age. He started in property management at the age of 16, and from that moment on, TJ knew he would work in the real estate industry, in some capacity. TJ's love for real estate lead to him obtaining his degree from the University of Wisconsin-Whitewater, with a degree in Finance and emphasis on Real Estate. Shortly after graduation in 2005, TJ obtained his Real Estate license and hasn't looked back. While TJ has focused solely on residential real estate, you will also find him investing in his own rental properties and helping others see the benefit of owning residential income property.

TJ is the founder of Strategic Real Estate Experts and is constantly pushing the envelope on what is possible when helping home buyers and sellers. Spend a few minutes talking to him and you will see his passion come through for truly making a difference in the lives he comes into contact with. TJ says, "It's not just about doing a deal, it's about truly making a positive impact on the lives we touch and putting the buyers and sellers we help in the best position possible when the time comes to make a move."

TJ's real estate career started at a young age but that hasn't stopped him from enjoying some time away from work with people he cares about. While TJ is passionate about changing the Real Estate industry, you'll also find him spending time with his family, coaching youth hockey, playing softball, seeing the fall colors in northern Wisconsin and having his nieces and nephews over to visit. TJ says he also really enjoys that Jesus fella and spending any free time with Big V (his dad) and Bitsy. Special thanks should also go out to Shawn, Ryan, his friend Ted, and everyone else who has been a part of his life, including his Mom (Robin) and Stepdad (Greg). According to some, TJ is deep down a kid at heart and loves life to the fullest.

You can connect with TJ at:

- https://www.facebook.com/tjvitense
- https://www.instagram.com/tjvitense/
- tj@sreehelp.com

CHAPTER 11

THE TIPPING POINT OF SUCCESS — A NEW MODEL A NEW WAY

BY LARS LOFSTRAND

Dead! Dead! Dead!

Dead I tell you!

The traditional Real Estate Brokerage model is Dead!

By traditional, I mean that the model of bringing on agents for a 'blanket' across the board split and bringing them in to teach them how to be a better agent is dead! Brokerages have been doing this for more years than most people can remember. Although the model has been tweaked slightly, the fundamental formula has remained the same.

Agents are brought in fresh out of Real Estate School, 10%, 20%, 30% even up to 50% taken off the top as the brokerage split for allowing the agent the privilege of hanging their license at the brokerage, with zero or nothing much being given in return for the split. What's more, they are then sold further training and development to help further them in becoming competent Real

Estate Agents, teaching them how to own a job.

In short, brokerages have become no more than training and development companies pedaling their wares, selling agents more and more knowledge. The challenge is that agents end up having more knowledge than they can use. That is the difference between education and training. Training implies hands on approach - a doing, not merely a knowing. Learning how to do it is more important than merely knowing what you should be doing. In fact, just knowing can lead to huge frustration.

Now, you know what you should be doing, but your failure to apply that knowledge leads to disappointment and feelings of inadequacy and regret. Knowledge doesn't equate to more success, the application of knowledge does. So, giving knowledge vs. teaching people how to use it becomes the Tipping Point of Success.

Business has fundamentally changed in the last decade and with it, how we run our businesses. We need to change or suffer the risk of being left behind. I've travelled the world asking business leaders the question:

"What is the Purpose of a business?"

To which nine times out of ten I get the reply: "To make Money!"

This is not only incorrect, but also grossly overrated, and directly affects how we run our businesses. I believe Peter Drucker, the late management guru, said it best. He said that the purpose of a business was not to make money but rather – "To satisfy a client." I have gone one further and added: "To create and to satisfy a client."

The reason I added the create part in is because most clients don't know what it is that they need and want, and as a result this allows the unique opportunity for us to take them through a discovery process, and for that need and want to be created. It is near impossible to satisfy a client if they don't feel they have a need or a want for what it is that you have. Therefore the create portion becomes critical to the satisfying element.

Does this mean to say that Money is not important? No! Money is essential, but it is not the purpose of a business. So, what is money then? Money is simply the measure of how well you are doing towards the purpose. Focus on satisfying the customer and the money will follow automatically. The greater the customer satisfaction, the greater the return or measure of money.

So why the importance of sharing this with you? Well, firstly it is important to know that the most important person in your business is the customer, and satisfying this customer becomes essential for your business not only to thrive but to survive. Studies show that the majority of business start-ups fail within the first few years, so to win in business we need to learn this principal of focus as soon as possible.

Now brokerages have been around forever, and just because the traditional model is dead doesn’t mean that they will disappear any time soon, but it's important to know that most businesses are working ‘way too hard’ trying to attract and to maintain and retain top performers. The real estate industry has a high percentage of people turnover which costs huge amounts of money, and in turn, affects bottom lines around the world.

I believe that this turnover occurs when agents figure out that they are not getting much for the split they pay, or the mere fact that they come to a realization that they are not feeding their families as they are not doing the required business in order to be successful, and this all as a result of not knowing what to do – as there is very little help from other agents they are surrounded by.

Why?

This is because the other agents are too busy trying to make ends meet themselves. The time is long overdue to create a model that breed's synergy between agents – a model where it is a pay-to-play scenario and not merely an across the board fixed-split percentage.

The reason seasoned agents don't help the newer agents is firstly, they don't have the time. The reason they don't give the time or limit the time they give is because time is literally money, and if the time they sacrifice does not relate to dollars, it would not only be foolish to sacrifice the time, but also detrimental to their business.

Getting agents to be more productive is a critical part of growing a brokerage. I believe that a new model is overdue. A model where we teach agents how to run a business, rather than merely teaching them how to be good agents which essentially keeps them 'employed' or 'self employed' at best. I regularly joke that agents are called brokers because they usually are broker than everyone else.

A new model is required that teaches agents how a successful business works. Agents need a model that teaches agents to work together, to support each other and to capitalize on the strengths of those around them. They need a model that does all this, and at the same time, compensates them for the sacrificed time.

I've always said that there are only three things you have in any business, and learning to leverage these three things is critical to growing a sustainable business –not only in the Real Estate industry, but in any and all industries. Learning to 'let go' therefore becomes a critical element in harnessing the power of synergy.

I call these three things the 3 T's. They are namely:

1. Time.
2. Talent.
3. Treasure.

1. **Time** – is something that we, as humans, all have an equal amount – no more, no less. It doesn't matter how well you manage time you won't get more of it, as there are only 24 hours in a day. In fact, my father always taught me that you can lose and waste money and always make more. However, if you waste time, it can never be replaced. Therefore, time is the most precious resource we have. Yet it's the resource we waste the most of. We are quick to try to save a dollar, but quick to give the time away to create that dollar, and in my consulting experience I've seen how many people and businesses are operating at a loss and they don't even realize it.

2. **Talent** – is people and the skills you need to run a business. No one is irreplaceable and you can always find people to do the things you need done.

3. **Treasure** – is Money. Money is similar to people. It is merely a resource that you can make or get. They say if you need it, you can find money and you can find people.

My father always said to me: "Son, you if you lose talent, you can always replace it. If you lose money you can always make more, but if you waste time you will never get it back again."

With that being said, our focus should be on the most precious resource we have: Time. We need to learn how to save it, use it, spend it, invest in it and to leverage it in order to get more done. The traditional real estate brokerage model does not teach us how to use it effectively. In fact, most brokerages teach us how to be better agents and how to better do what is required to be a good agent. Therefore, keeping us captive to the time we have.

We should not be teaching realtors how to be better agents and how to do more stuff, but rather how to get rid of the stuff that needs to be done – especially the stuff we are no good at or the stuff that we are weak at – which will free us up to focus on what we are good at and what we can do well. We need to learn how to work 'on' our business and not 'in' our business.

I have been training and coaching in the Real Estate Business for over 15 years and I've observed how agents get stuck in a rut of feast-or-famine and that cycle is typically 3 months of feast followed by 3 months of famine. For example: while you are servicing and showing clients you are not lead generating, while you are doing admin. you are not following up with past clients, etc., etc.

Over the years of observing the habits of realtors and working with them on honing their skills, I have observed that as human beings we are good at some things and bad at others. I have thus determined that we need to do the things we are good at and get rid of the rest.

Below, you will find a model that you can follow to learn what needs to be done in a transaction from start to finish. We need to learn to give tasks away, and this is not easy to do if you don't know what goes on in a Real Estate transaction. Herewith are my recommendations of what needs to be done. You need to study the tasks that a Real Estate transaction requires, and figure out which ones you like doing and what you're good at, vs the things you don't like to do and that you are not good at.

The items below become somewhat of a budget you need and will use to manage your real estate business.

THE NEW MODEL

So, assume that after your Broker transaction fee or split, which is your cost of doing business, what is left will represent 100% of your net earned income, from that the following percentages will be allocated to the various aspects of a real estate transaction. Get with some other agent and figure out what you are going to give away to them and what you are going to keep. They will only get paid based on a percentage of the deal when it closes. I believe this is the best way to do it as it creates an entrepreneurial model that holds everyone accountable and makes sure that there are no weak links in the chain, as every person on the team will need to perform their part in order for the deal to close. Remember that all these various items represent a job that has to be done. Now you can do them all yourself or you can learn to outsource them.

SELLER SIDE:

20% Care – This is the portion that looks within the business. Things that make the business run smoother, like systems and training and development.

Breakdown of the Care:

- Text/Email support
- Fast Track training
- Boot-Camp training
- Sales Systems
- Admin. Tools

20% Create - creation of lead. Lead generation. You can use this to buy leads or to market to get your own leads.

5% Convert – converting a lead to appointment. This position can be given to someone who is good at inside sales.

5% Commit – getting a lead to commit to signing a listing agreement with you to sell their home.

5% Coordinate – this portion goes to a transaction coordinator who will do all the admin from the time of going under contract to close.

25% Captivate – this is the portion that goes to the process of marketing property.

Breakdown of 25% Captivate:

- 2.5% Pulling the CMA's.
- 2.5% Inputting the data into the MLS.
- 5% Measure and collect data on the home.
- 5% Property Website.
- 5% Open House Marketing to make sure the house gets held open.
- 2.5% Installation of the Sign and Lockbox.
- 2.5% Attend Closing at the end of the transaction.

5% Compliance – making sure the paperwork is all in compliance.

15% Close - negotiate and facilitate the transaction to close.

BUYER SIDE:

20% Care - This is the portion that looks within the business. Things that make the business run smoother, like systems and training and development.

Breakdown of the Care:

- Text/Email Support
- Fast Track Training
- Boot-Camp Training
- Sales Systems
- Admin. Tools

20% Create - creation of lead. Lead generation. You can use this to buy leads or to market to get your own leads.

5% Convert – converting a lead to appointment. This position can be given to someone who is good at inside sales.

5% Commit – getting a lead to commit to signing a buyer's representation with you to find them a home.

5% Coordinate – this portion goes to a transaction coordinator who will do all the admin from the time of going under contract to close.

25% Captivate – this is the portion that goes to the process of showing property.

Breakdown of 25% Captivate:

- 2.5% Pull the CMA's.
- 2.5% Showing: Opening Doors only.
- 15% Showing: Qualifying the Client as well as opening doors.
- 2.5% Setup of Appointments to show homes.
- 2.5% Attend Closing at the end of the transaction.

5% Compliance – making sure the paperwork is all in compliance.
15% Close - negotiate and facilitate the transaction to close.

From the above you can see that there is more than one thing that goes into having a successful transaction.

Study the above breakdown of the New Model and, as I said earlier, figure out what you need to be doing and what you need to be giving away.

Good Luck and Happy House Hunting.

About Lars

Lars Lofstrand is what is known as a “Serial Entrepreneur,” having started, owned and run 19 different businesses. He is passionate about business and helping other entrepreneurs and people wanting to be entrepreneurs realize their dream of owning a successful business.

Through his speaking, seminars, workshops, books, CDs and consulting, he travels the world teaching that health, wealth, happiness and peace of mind are possible for all who desire it. Lars reveals his secrets to having a successful business and how you can conquer the 8 areas of your life, to harness the power of thought, putting your dreams into action, to live a more rewarding life, a life of abundance and Success.

Lars became a business success at an early age, transforming into a respected leadership authority, author, talented teacher, speaker, futurist and organizational consultant, having gained much and lost everything, in many business ventures.

Lars was Qualified and trained as a Psychological Profiler in Waco, Texas and is the author of the bestselling book *Sticky Money.*

People consistently rate Lars Löfstrand as the top speaker, facilitator and consultant at conferences, seminars, coaching and training sessions around the globe. He has an appeal that transcends barriers of age, culture and occupation. His laid back and humorous style ensures that his message is not only heard and remembered but put into action long after the event has come to an end.

[Logon to: www.capacitycompany.com to get free in-depth video tutorials and trainings on how to use and implement the New Model.]

CHAPTER 12

STRATEGY OR STRATEGY – NO OTHER OPTION

BY DOMINGO RODRIGUEZ

Opportunity knocks on our door all the time, we just need to be present for each moment to understand the offering. It was a bit too late when I eventually understood how strategic and masterful my mother was at living her life while raising me as a single parent.

When I was fourteen, my mom dropped me off at my school to get on the bus for my basketball game. That day she was struggling a bit with her asthma. "You don't sound well Mom, maybe you should go to the hospital," I said. After all, it was only down the hill. She smiled then waved goodbye and took off. As I watched her pull away expecting her to head down the hill, she headed towards home instead. I stood still in disappointment for a minute wondering why she was being so stubborn. Thereafter we were told the game was cancelled due to snow, so I walked home. As I approached my house walking through the playground, one of my neighbor's frantically ran toward me saying, "Your mom passed out and doesn't look good." I sprinted as fast as I could and made my way to go help her, I saw she was not breathing; I was pushed out the way, paramedics began CPR. Two short minutes later she was gone forever.

I was in absolute shock as my world came crumbling down in this brief instance. I didn't know where to turn or what to do, I locked myself in the bathroom for hours. Family members came to our house and they all asked for me, but I was silently sitting in my anguish feeling isolated and alone. Finally there was a knock at the bathroom door, it was my oldest cousin, "Junior, you plan on staying in there forever?" I didn't answer. He then said the words that changed my life forever, "You know your mother would not want you to be like this, she would want you to be happy." And this resonated within me. I felt myself coming out of the catatonic state I'd been in those last few hours. I opened the door, little did I know I was stepping out into a whole new life.

MOVING ON AND GOING FORWARD

After my mom passed, my older sister and her two children came from Colombia to move in with me. It was a challenging time being an adolescent with no parents. Shortly after that I had a few run-ins with the law which made my sister believe I would not be a good influence on her children. There were many occasions where her treatment toward me began to change. I knew it was bad, I'd get home from school and there was nothing for me to eat and I went to bed hungry. I kept myself occupied with school and sports while supporting myself by working. It was during this time I realized I needed strategies to juggle all of this at one time. I always had a following due to my innate social skills. I was able to utilize this to my advantage. I began to understand the power of having a strategy in place.

"Some day you will be a college student," my mother repeated over and over. One day a friend told me he had a brilliant fool-proof plan to skip a few classes without getting caught. The plan was go to the college recruiter event hosted by our school, we would ask for a pass to attend the event and leave school thereafter. We showed up at the event and to our horror we were the only two students there, standing in front of the college recruiter. They asked us both questions and quickly helped each of us fill out an application. The recruiter stated she was able to give us acceptance results right at that moment. "Domingo, you are in, and Robert you are out," she stated. I was shocked!

I was definitely not planning on filling out college applications let alone get accepted to one. The school was looking for certain criteria for their Equal Opportunity Program, and I was it, low income and average grades. Amazing how a brilliant strategic move to cut class led me to the opportunity of being admitted into college. During the next four years at a college campus, I matured in ways I never imagined, my social abilities flourished and I gained access to, and leveraged, many things an average student would not experience. I starred in lead roles in plays, was homecoming king, I became the concert chairman of the college and developed a blueprint still used to this day for hosting major events.

Soon after graduating, I worked in the music industry for MCA records as a Marketing Manager. I was the liaison between the music stores and the MCA label. I consistently worked hand in hand with artists such as the late BB King, Patty LaBelle, Sublime, The Ramones, and Mary J. Blige to name a few. My position kept me active by continuously working on creative marketing ideas for each artist and their specific needs. Strategy became my way of life, especially if I wanted to impress not only the artist, but also the major record executives. As time went on, the music industry changed and giant mergers became the norm, shrinking many positions out of the record labels. Nonetheless, another opportunity was granted even if I was sent home with a severance package. Strategy strikes again!

Change is often unwelcome – it is up to the individual to roll out the welcome mat and invite it in for coffee.

One beautiful sunny summer day I had scheduled an appointment to preview an apartment. On my way there, I saw a sign for a moving sale. I decided to take a look and began to talk with the current tenants, who were moving out of state and selling quite a bit of their belongings. Looking at their items for sale, I was more interested in their bright and spacious apartment. They told me the landlord was hosting an open house on Sunday and I should come back to meet him. I did just that, but to my surprise, there were 25 other people there at the same time all interested in that apartment.

At that moment I had an epiphany, and said to myself, "Wow, real estate must be good!" That evening I called my uncle, asking how someone could get involved working in real estate and he mentioned that he has seen ads in newspapers for real estate courses. The very next morning on my way to work, I passed a newspaper stand and remembered the conversation I had with my uncle the night before. Newspaper! I opened the newspaper and there it was: a big ad for obtaining a Real Estate license. In that moment something unexplainable came over me and I made the call. As I look back, I realize the strategies I created for myself were being aware and taking immediate action – which has led me to an illustrious seventeen-year career in real estate.

SUCCESS IS DETERMINED BY YOUR HEART'S VALUE, NOT DESIRE

True strategy is the comprehension of human needs. In order to serve others you must first understand their values. This is by far the most critical aspect of helping your clients, so that the direction and pace at which you work with them provides a meaningful journey when they are selling or purchasing a home.

1. **Ensure you get expert advice from a full-time Realtor, with a proven track record.**
   Let me give you a vivid example, let's say you needed open-heart surgery and you were looking to select a surgeon, would you hire a surgeon that works another job and performs only a few operations each year, or a surgeon that performs hundreds per year with a high success rate and is

always in demand. The same principle applies to a Realtor handling one of the biggest assets you will ever acquire in your life.

2. **Look for an expert based on your specific transaction needs.**
   Different transactions require unique knowledge and expertise. A few examples of these might be a simultaneous sell and purchase, relocation, an out-of-state owner or a short sale, etc. For these, a Realtor would need to take courses above and beyond the required continuing education classes and the ability to demonstrate they can service these types of transactions.

3. **Require an Action Plan.**
   Ensure you have an understanding of what to expect throughout the course of the transaction prior to, during contract and at closing. The plan should be transparent, feasible, measureable and above all, flexible.

4. **Consider hiring a real estate team that leverages people and systems as compared to an individual agent.**
   As the old cliché goes, there's power in numbers! A real estate team supports every aspect of your transaction. In today's market, to achieve maximum results it takes a group of experts to get the job done. There is always someone available and each team member works in an area they are most passionate about – allowing them to perform at a high level. Personalized service from a team of experts allows for a faster, smoother, high-quality real estate experience.

THE NOW

I am fortunate to have become a Realtor and experience all the blessings I have, thus far. Through the many challenges in my life I have always been led to opportunities that called for some sort of strategic thinking to continuously move ahead. As I continue my journey, I consistently give back to my community by serving on my church board, coaching football, and motivational speaking to children and young adults. It is through community that we build our wealth; real estate just happens to be a personal passion of mine.

About Domingo

Domingo Rodriguez is a visionary and motivated leader that always expresses gratitude for his deep roots – being born and raised in Passaic, New Jersey. Attending Martin Luther King #6 school, then Lincoln Middle School, he graduated from Passaic High School, class of 1990, and then graduated with his Bachelor's Degree, majoring in Communications, from William Paterson University. Domingo has preserved many personal obstacles; he has had to deal with the loss of his mother at the young age of 14 and always dealt with an absentee father. Born to parents who were immigrants from their own country, the Dominican Republic and Colombia, Domingo has been equipped from a young age to embrace the use of both languages fluently and learned to seek the true value of family.

As we fast forward in life now, Domingo has been in the real estate business for 16 years, earning his license in 2000 and broker's license in 2004. With a team of agents and himself, Domingo is employed with Re/Max Executive Group in Hawthorne, NJ. His career is solely built from referrals through past clients and acquaintances that appreciate best practice and expertise for the real estate market.

Domingo has been married since 2007 and has two children. Domingo is dedicated to sharing his story with many people of all ages who can understand that life is about pressing hard no matter what circumstances you encounter. His message is understood loud and clear, and because of this, he has been honorably recommended to speak for many years at Lincoln Middle School in Passaic, Rafael Fernandez Elementary School in Newark, and to other local organizations. His will to inspire and move people is a gift and a great legacy he plans to build upon in the near future.

CHAPTER 13

THE "LIFE FACTOR"

BY BC RISI

So here you are and I'm sure that you must be wondering about the title of this chapter? My purpose for this chapter and what I wanted to share with you is a simple concept. The "LIFE FACTOR" is a combination of all the things in total that affect our daily lives. It is every bit of the diversity that has an impact on all of us each and every day, and gets in the way or holds us back. You see, if I can do it, so can you!

Each of us has our own "LIFE FACTOR" to deal with. It is the set of circumstances in our daily lives which impacts us, shapes and molds us into who we ultimately are or are not. If we don't intervene and take control of the chaos, it can completely and utterly defeat us. What I have learned from other successful people is that they have learned and conditioned themselves to use any of this negative adversity to their advantage. They do that by using it to inspire, motivate and propel themselves into tremendous action. So, what is it that really makes the difference as to which road a person chooses? It is a choice after all. Right?

Sharing just a few of these things might just help you to know that you are not the only one dealing with the "LIFE FACTOR". While your days seemingly are filled with distraction addictions that prevent you from making progress, these gigantic hurdles and impossibilities can be conquered. . . and that you too can accomplish anything you set your mind to, in spite of whatever "LIFE FACTOR" you have been dealt!

Do you understand clearly that it is not only you and I? How many times during the day, the month, year and even in your life have you noticed someone else's "LIFE FACTOR"? How many times do we have a "head-turning event" and massive realization or epiphany in thought? Everybody has the same 24 hours in a day. Yet, some people have risen above insurmountable circumstances and their "LIFE FACTORS". How does any of this relate to real estate?

First of all, let's ask the right questions? Is having a successful, productive and more meaningful personal life a priority to you? Do you want to have a more successful real estate business? How important is your self-talk? Does your attitude play a significant role? Did you know that it all comes down to you? How important is it to have realistic yet progressive and even edgy expectations? It is a decision that will start the engine or not!! Right?

So let me share a little information with you about someone famous. This is a typical and similar failure-to-success ratio shared by so many of the successful people I've had the pleasure of meeting and interacting with. This man spent more than 30 years of difficult diversity, multitudes of failures, and few successes along the way – before reaching the pinnacle of his professional success. Check this out . . .

- 1831 - Lost his job – age 22
- 1832 - Defeated in his run for Illinois State Legislature – age 23
- 1833 - Failed in business and Filed Bankruptcy – age 24
- 1834 - Elected to Illinois State Legislature – age 25
- 1835 - Long time Sweetheart died – age 26
- 1836 - Had a Nervous Breakdown – age 27
- 1838 - Defeated in run for Illinois House Speaker – age 29

- 1843 - Defeated in run for Nomination for U.S. Congress – age 34
- 1846 - Elected to Congress – age 37
- 1848 - Lost his Re-Nomination to Congress – age 39
- 1849 - Rejected for Land Officer Position – age 40
- 1854 - Defeated in his run for U.S. Senate – age 45
- 1856 - Defeated in his run for Nomination for Vice President of the United States – age 47
- 1858 - Again defeated in his run for U.S. Senate – age 49
- 1860 - Elected President of the United States – age 51

Thirty years of trying relentlessly before being elected President of the United States. We are talking about Abraham Lincoln. Did you know that there are stories after stories just like this one?—where somebody overcame all the odds and everything thrown at them – only to succeed.

Well, let's dig into some of this. I am anxious to share with you a few of the things that I've learned along the way on my journey; this incredible journey of life and all the "LIFE FACTORS" that none of us can completely escape however; we can overcome and find success, peace, harmony and yes … satisfaction in our lives.

I guarantee that anybody that has achieved a high level of success in their life had a few circumstances involving "LIFE FACTORS." If you are anything like me, I always wondered how people did it? How did they rise above their own circumstances and all the predicament's we get into? Are you one of these people? Maybe you have these circumstances going on right now:

- Single Parent
- Single Parent with Multiple Kids
- Transportation Issues
- Lack of Experience
- Divorced People
- Family Problems

- Busy Trying to Survive
- Financial Challenges
- No Finances
- Special Needs
- Credit Challenges
- No Credit
- Health Issues
- Environment concerns, like where you live
- Out-of-Shape People
- Child Support
- Bankruptcy
- Negative Surroundings
- Negative People in your Life
- Lack of Motivation
- No Role Models
- etc., etc., etc.

So what is the secret that those successful people know and how do they do it? You know, I've realized over the years that it really was not as complicated as I had originally thought. In fact, it's really simple and very basic. The things that make the difference, that is! I am about to share a list of 15 things that I've learned and been using for some time now.

If you take these seriously and go step-by-step, one-by-one, expanding the topic and then begin incorporating what you learn . . . your real estate business and personal life will be unrecognizable in a positive way one year from now. Imagine three or five years from now. There is a difference between "Working On" your life and just "Living your Life." There is also a big difference between "Working On" your business and "Working In" your business.

If the right things are repeated over and over again with diligence, persistence and relentless pursuit that is compounded over time . . . the roadway of your success will be paved and undeniable.

These are not in any kind of priority order, but I look at them like the spokes on a wheel. Each spoke is equally important to the performance of the entire wheel. Just like the spokes on a wheel, each spoke must be properly tightened, aligned and balanced for the wheel to roll at high speeds properly. We are no different than the wheel when we are out of balance. Here you go . . .

1) ***Don't Reinvent the Wheel:*** Which is easier? Learning on your own, or learning from somebody else that is already there doing it? When you want to effect a change in yourself or develop a new habit . . . go seek out those already doing it and use them as a role model. There are lots of ways to do this. Make sure you choose your Role Models wisely.

2) ***Feed your Internal Self for Personal Growth, Learning and Mindset:*** Always review and saturate yourself with the right material. Associate with and work around people conducive to the direction you want to go. This would include but not be limited to books, eBooks, audio books, pertinent seminars, mentors, coaches, professional peers. Don't be afraid to immerse yourself in and around everything and everybody that is already where you want to go. If there is one thing that sticks out for me in all my experiences, it's that most successful people genuinely want to help, and very much enjoy helping, sincere people.

3) ***Feed your Outside Physical Self:*** Your physical health and conditioning (i.e., exercise, diet) is equally important. This is not an option . . . it's mandatory!!

4) ***Maintain a Positive Self Image:*** See yourself already where you want to be. Take time to make time . . . and Make time to be there! I go through a ritual every morning straight out of bed and every evening before getting into bed. I have something that I recite to myself that is near and dear to my heart and has tremendous value to me. It goes like this: *"BC conducts his daily life with absolute integrity, loyalty*

and compassion. He nurtures and cares for his children and serves his clients diligently, resulting in his complete happiness." This takes less than 30 seconds. You may be surprised how something so simple can be so powerful and have a positive and dramatic impact your life.

5) ***Maintain a Positive Can Do Attitude:*** Do you live in "Vision" or "Circumstances"? Are you a "Victim" of circumstances or a "Victor" of circumstances? Attitude determines your Altitude.

6) ***About Problems:*** Be an expert at "Identifying" the problems AND ALSO AN EXPERT AT "Finding the Solutions" to the problems.

7) ***Flip The Script:*** What I've noticed about most successful people is that they have taught themselves how to take the negatives and flip them into positives. When a negative thought enters your mind take it and quickly think of three positive things. Guess what? It works!! Learn to Flip that Script!

8) ***Systemize and Automate:*** This is where we get back to the spokes on the wheel and the importance of all of them being properly tightened and balanced. A simple strategy is to first identify everything in the process you want to systemize. Then identify those parts that are not working well. Figure out some new ways for those parts to work well and continue doing this process until literally every moving part has been identified. A simple example of this might be the part of your real estate business that concerns signs and lockboxes. These are the stages of both:
    1. Sign goes up;
    2. Lockbox goes up;
    3. Sign Riders (Coming Soon, For Sale, Pending & Sold) need to be rotated during the transaction;
    4. Sign goes down;

5. Lockbox goes down;
6. Track all of this so current status is readily available.

So, what is the current process like? Usually this is the agent doing everything. In my case with a high-volume brokerage, it is not feasible for me to be involved with this process. So in my case I have employed somebody in-house to manage the entire process for a flat fee per transaction. Once they get the order, they manage it from the beginning to the end. I pay them upon closing just like the rest of us are paid. I don't have to touch any part of it because a system has been put in place so that I don't have to be there for it to be done. I wrestled over this one thing for so long before I finally took the time to develop the system that I now have in place.

9) ***Communication:*** Frequent, Precise and Accurate communications. Especially in the Real Estate Industry. Absence of or poor communication leads to confusion. Confusion is stressful, wastes time, delays closings and nothing good comes out of it. Bad communication is also a Morale Killer.

10) ***Extreme Patience and Delayed Gratification:*** It has been said repeatedly that practicing patience can radically increase your capacity for successful results. There are so many payoffs to being patient – particularly when it has to do with the timing of things, costs and results. I could write a whole book on this topic because I was one of the least patient people I knew. Remember there is always time to do it twice, but never enough time to do it right the first time. Exercise patience in all that you do!!

11) ***Intense and Focused Planning:*** Nothing gets done without first taking the time to create a plan. Expecting results without a written plan is an expectation that will only let you down over and over again. Take the time to do this right. There are so many resources available on the internet. Find a technique that appeals to you and get it done.

12) ***Commit to Putting Things in Writing:*** Be willing to put your plans in writing. Know where you are at today and put it in writing. All your procedures, systems, actions and processes must be put in writing. That which is committed to paper can be improved. Track your results and put it in writing, otherwise how will you know whether there is progress or not. Did I say put it all in writing?

13) ***Don't Worry about What Other People Think:*** Be different and be yourself. Do not worry about what other people think about you! Fact is, if you are doing the right things and moving your business in the right direction … there will probably be a few people that are not happy with you.

14) ***Be Deliberate about Everything:*** This is another one of those topics that goes deep, high, wide and far. I always picture in my mind the importance of this with two sayings I grew up with. If you start a very long journey and you start just one degree off. Does it make much of a difference after the first mile? How much of a difference does your ending destination make after 10,000 miles? Maybe this will be a better illustration and analogy. If the archer misses the target, is it ever the targets fault? Be very deliberate and precise with everything you do in both your Personal Life and your Real Estate Business.

15) ***Fall in Love with all your Clients:*** What I mean is that just like the love you show your children or friends – where you take your time, give your time and are compassionate in your consideration and service to them. Remember while you may have done a certain thing like list a property for sale a thousand times before; it may be the clients very first time. So be gentle, caring and loving.

In closing, I want to wish each and every one of you the very best in all your endeavors. Sometimes the simplest of things can seem like the hardest things. All fifteen of these nuggets have been time-tested and proven by hundreds if not thousands of people before you and me. Take each one and explore it thoroughly and put it to work for you. Watch what happens. A journey of 10,000 miles begins with the first step. Take your first step!!

About BC

BC Risi, as a single parent of four children with three currently at home, operates a full-time and very busy Real Estate business as well. BC conducts his daily life with absolute integrity, loyalty and compassion. He nurtures and cares for his children and serves his clients diligently resulting in his complete happiness.

BC grew up as a product of a career Air Force family that moved quite frequently around the U.S., Germany and Japan during his earlier years. His parents divorced at age 11.

BC, being the oldest of five children, remained with his mother and four younger siblings. BC moved out of his mother's home at age 14. At age 15, he graduated high school and started working in the Movie Industry doing lighting on movie sets. He started college and he eventually became a lighting director (gaffer) by age 19. The seasonality of the industry provided many other opportunities for BC – like getting a real estate license and earning his bachelor's degree.

Today BC is a licensed Trusted Expert Real Estate Advisor who has spent 42 years perfecting his craft, serving his clients at the highest levels. BC has enjoyed with frequency thousands of successes for his clients, while helping them to achieve goals that others said could not be done. In California, BC launched a Real Estate and Mortgage Loan company that quickly grew to nine offices throughout the state, had over 600 real estate agents and loan officers which took just four short years. Today BC is quickly re-establishing himself in his market as an Expert Advisor for Home Services and a major player in that market.

BC currently holds an active Brokers License in California and an active Salesperson's License in Texas where he now resides. BC's commitment to service, self-improvement, professionalism, education within the industry and immense enthusiasm for his clients and the work that he does is noticed. His contagious positive attitude and high energy has enabled him to consistently exceed expectations with his clients as a result.

BC is an active participant in North Texas real estate as a member of the

National Association of Realtors, The Texas Association of Realtors and the Collin County Association of Realtors. He is a member in good standing of NAEA the National Association of Expert Advisors. BC's clients expect, deserve and receive access to the latest leading-edge technologies to obtain maximum exposure in the market place, so that they can quickly and efficiently navigate to their goals.

BC loves public speaking, educating and working with his community and the public about his industry, is an expert in Martial Arts, a Private Pilot and loves to ride his motorcycle.

His motto is . . .

SKILL, INTEGRITY & PERSEVERANCE!!
Building A Brighter Future!! One Dream at A Time!!

You can connect with BC at:

- Email: BC.Risi@ExpertAdvisor.com or BCRisiRE@gmail.com
- https://www.facebook.com/BCRisiExpertRealEstateAdvisors/?fref=ts
- https://twitter.com/BCRisi
- www.BCRisi.com

CHAPTER 14

THE EXPERT DIFFERENCE

BY LANDON WARD

The Lehman's have finally decided to sell their home. After months and months of deciding on whether they should sell, they finally put the sign in the front yard. "FOR SALE BY OWNER", the sign reads, with their phone number proudly displayed underneath. Terry nails the post into the front lawn, adjusts the sign so it is easy to see from the road, and heads back inside to sit down and wait for the calls to come flooding in. The market is moving quickly and their neighbor just got a great offer and are under contract.

"If THAT house can sell so fast, ours should sell even FASTER, right?" he mutters jokingly to his wife Karen.

Karen with a chuckle responded quickly, "Oh, definitely."

Terry was right, the calls DID come in. What he wasn't expecting was that the calls coming in were from other agents promising that they had "interested buyers." He jumped at the opportunity to show the house to the agents. One after another they came to see the house. No offers. Terry quickly realized all the agents wanted to do was list their home, they didn't have any buyers. He started getting the feeling that those agents needed to sell his home more than he and Karen did.

After a couple months of trying to sell on their own, and ANOTHER home in the neighborhood on the market was quickly brought under contract, Karen sat down with Terry to talk. Karen was concerned that they were never going to sell. They had shown the home to a couple of different buyers that called the number on their sign and internet ad, but they weren't serious buyers. They just wanted to look at homes. "Why don't we just list our house with one of those agents that came to see our house last month?" she asked. Terry responded, "Why would we list with someone who needs to sell our home more than we do? We will sell. Just be patient." Karen was frustrated. All the time they had spent showing "buyers" the home, all the time making sure the home was in tip-top shape with two young children at home, she finally wanted an answer. Karen noticed the neighbors loading the moving truck and quickly ran outside to say goodbye.

While helping load a couple of small boxes, she asked her neighbor Cindy a question, "How were you able to sell your home so fast?"

Cindy responded, "We hired an Expert Advisor®."

After Cindy briefly explained what an Expert Advisor® was and how they got their home sold so quickly and for top dollar, she rushed back in to tell Terry. Terry was on the phone with yet another agent that wanted to "preview" the home for his buyers. He knew EXACTLY what the agent wanted. It was the same story as all the other agents. Frustrated, he hangs up the phone. Karen notices the call didn't go well.

"Hey Terry?" she asks.

"Yeah?" he responds.

"Cindy told me they hired an Expert Advisor®," Karen said.

Terry responded, "What the heck is that?"

Karen then explained to Terry that an Expert Advisor® is:

"Someone who has a proven and repeatable system, backed by market research to sell your home for up to 18% more money™ than traditional real estate agents."

She then hands him a business card that Cindy gave to her with an Expert Advisor® on it. He begrudgingly picks up the phone to call.

Terry called and got in touch with the Expert Advisor® and noticed something very different almost immediately. He was asking questions about what THEY wanted and needed and why THEY needed to move. The Advisor genuinely wanted to help, and started to help 'game plan' with Terry what steps were necessary to get them to their end goal. Terry was excited, and couldn't wait to tell Karen about the details of the conversation. After sitting down with the Expert Advisor®, Karen and Terry decided to list their home.

After a week and a half goes by with their home listed with their Expert Advisor®, they put "Under Contract" on the sign. They had finally done it. They finally sold their home. After two months of nothing but frustration and wasted time trying to go it alone, their Advisor got it sold quickly and for more than asking price! They were convinced that if they hadn't hired an Expert they would have had to settle for less.

Stories like these are common in today's market. Home sellers commonly believe that if they sell their home themselves, they will net more money. While selling on your own can allow you to save some money, this is the rare exception. Going it alone is asking for disappointment and frustration. While selling your home on your own can cause undue stress and wasted time and effort, so too can hiring your average frustrated real estate agent. Like Terry's experience in this story, many other sellers have expressed similar dealings with agents. They felt as if the agent needed to sell their home more than they themselves did.

Through research and experiences with others just like the Lehman's, we have identified seven laws that make up our Expert Advisor® Smart Home Selling System. This is, "A proven, repeatable system, backed by market research to sell your home for up to 18% more money™ than traditional real estate agents." These seven laws are the playbook used to be able to sell homes for the most amount of money in the least amount of time. While there are seven laws in total and they all work congruently, I want to speak specifically about the first three laws. Those are, 1) The Law of Expertise, 2) The Law of Differentiation, and 3) The Law of Exposure.

1. **The Law of Expertise:**

   In the Law of Expertise, we have identified that many home sellers are so caught up in the sales price that they tend to forget their goals. An Expert Advisor® cares about your goals and sincerely wants you to meet and exceed those goals as quickly as possible. We have a saying in our office that we want our clients to understand – "Giving you a price before analysis is like a Doctor giving you a prescription before making a diagnosis." The starting point for our analysis happens when we ask you The Hard Questions™. Questions like:

   - What is your reason for selling and how soon are you looking to make a move?
   - What if the home doesn't sell, what would be your plan B?
   - What are your financial goals?
   - What are your past experiences with other agents?

   These specific questions aren't ground breaking, but you would be surprised at how many agents don't care to know this information because it doesn't directly benefit them. Again, it's all about providing the best possible experience and if we don't ask, we won't know how to best help you.

   The real estate industry is the only industry that looks at the PAST to determine FUTURE value. How crazy is that?

That is like trying to drive forward while looking in the rear-view mirror to determine where you should go. It just doesn't make sense. That is exactly why we do not use the CMA™ (Comparative Market Analysis) that other average agents use. The CMA doesn't take into consideration the sellers' motivation like a loss of job, divorce, if the property was inherited, or they were relocated for work and had already moved out. On top of that, it doesn't even consider the condition of the home, if it was staged properly, or has a dated interior. Why would you rely on a dated, ineffective strategy of pricing the most expensive purchase or sale most people will ever make? I know I wouldn't.

2. **The Law of Differentiation:**

This law is all about standing out in a sea of sameness. What makes YOUR home different when it is presented to market? When you work with an Expert Advisor® you get expert staging advice. Professionally staged homes can sell for 6-10% more money. Not only can a staged home sell for more money, staging has also been shown to decrease market time up to 50%. Above all else, it's about the attraction of higher offers from the start, it allows you to start any negotiation at the top rather than hoping a good offer comes in close to asking.

An Expert Advisor® will also do a quality of life upgrade analysis. This is an evaluation of any possible upgrades that substantially increase sales price. These are things like new flooring or countertops. Because of our relationships this will allow the work to be completed at the lowest price possible. These upgrades provide an increase in perceived value that drives up demand against strong competition. All upgrades need to be looked at through the eyes of your target market. What does your target market look for or expect to see in each price range, and does your home have those things?

The number one deal killer of real estate transactions is the inspection. An Expert Advisor® will have a professional pre-inspection done to identify any potential deal killers before buyer's set eyes on the property. This will save you time and money in the long run. Combining a pre-inspection with a home warranty will give your property a clean bill of health and gives the buyers more confidence. Confidence level and higher offers go hand in hand, the more confident you can make the buyers in your property, the better the offer.

3. **The Law of Exposure:**

The average agent makes an investment of $89 per month towards marketing and promotion. If that number seems surprisingly low, that is because it is. That is the AVERAGE, that means there are agents who spend more and some that spend less. That means that half of all the agents that are out there are spending less than $89 per month on marketing a property, that number also includes marketing themselves. Scary, right? When you think of marketing a $350k home for sale do you think $89 or less per month for all promotion and advertising is going to cut it? An Expert Advisor® spends far more than that, in upwards of thousands towards marketing and promotion in their business. More importantly it is spent where it matters. Utilizing a deep, not wide, market penetration strategy is of extreme importance.

Studies show that 92% of buyers are using the internet to find their homes. Expert Advisors® make sure to advertise in the highest traffic sites and utilize upgraded home profiles. The top five sites by traffic volume for real estate are Zillow, Realtor.com, Homes.com, Trulia, and Yahoo Real Estate. Of the three major search engines, Google, Yahoo, and Bing; 81% use Google, 12% use Yahoo, 6% use Bing. This is important because it gives a clear picture of where the advertising spend needs to happen.

> Everyone will agree that first impressions matter. The first showing of your home is going to occur online. After two weeks on the market your home begins to be covered up by new homes that have hit the market. That is why it is extremely important to make sure the home is properly staged for photos, and professional photography equipment is used. I can't tell you how many times I've worked with buyers that want to see a home because, "the photos look great." Photos matter. When you are selecting an agent to work with, make sure that professional photography will be used. It may seem like a no brainer, but you would be surprised how many sellers allow horrible photos to be used to market their home.

All of this leads me to one final point. When you are ready to sell your home, make a checklist. If your prospective agent doesn't meet these vital criteria, you are selling yourself short. This is the largest transaction you will probably ever make in your life. Would you go to an eye doctor when you need knee surgery just because they are also a doctor and might do the surgery cheaper, or would you go see a knee specialist? I know my answer. Just because there are a lot of real estate agents out there doesn't mean they are all experts. Choose an Expert Advisor®.

About Landon

Landon Ward is an Expert Advisor® and the founder of the Northwest Arkansas Real Estate Experts located in one of the fastest growing and most desirable regions in the nation. Never afraid to challenge the traditional thinking of people's ideas of success, Landon didn't finish college. It wasn't that he didn't understand the importance of such education, it was that he had a burning desire to show others that it wasn't the only way. Landon began his sales career in sporting goods retail where he would eventually become a general manager by the age of 20. Soon after, he began work in the consumer electronics and telecommunications industries, where he experienced immense success. At those various stops, he realized that his success had a common theme, his passion for providing a better service attracted those wanting to transact.

Landon's jump to the real estate industry has been no different. Always striving for more and challenging the status quo, he has found a better way of doing business. Landon builds lasting relationships with his clients, and cares more about their goals and successes than his own pocket book. He believes the real estate industry has too long been filled with average agents, doing average work, on most of their clients largest most stressful transactions they will probably endure. Since the beginning of his real estate career, Landon has aggressively sought out the best and brightest in the industry to establish a mentor relationship. Those relationships have culminated into his use of a proven and repeatable system backed by market research, to net homeowners up to 18% more money™.

Landon Ward is a husband and father, born and raised in Northwest Arkansas where he operates his real estate business today. He is a member of the National Association of Expert Advisors®. Landon is also an active member of his local church, loves spending time with friends and family, learning from others, and is passionate about University of Arkansas athletics.

You can connect with Landon Ward at:

- Landon@NorthwestArkansasProperty.com
- www.facebook.com/LandonWardNWAExpert

CHAPTER 15

SURVIVE TO THRIVE

BY ERIC PENARANDA

It was a beautiful 95 degree summer day in Orlando, not a cloud in the sky, sun shining bright, basically the perfect day to start my career as a full time commercial real estate broker. I landed an excellent position with an international firm specializing in commercial real estate. My commute included a half mile walk to the downtown office wearing a suit and tie. The year is 2009; the Great Recession was well underway and happens to be the most catastrophic time period for commercial real estate in recent history.

The salary was zero; 100% of revenue was created by commission through effecting real estate transactions, so I eat only what I kill. My medical benefits included Dayquil and vitamin C boost packets conveniently located in the office kitchen. The perks were a phone, desk, some pens and air conditioning.

Sound dreadful? At the time, sure it was painful. Would I trade this experience for a cushy job, perks and not a worry in the world? Absolutely not.

The truth is prior to 2009, I held an incredible position developing real estate; my resume and project portfolio looked incredible on paper. My career seemed at the time to be headed for greatness and I could only look forward, yet I never took a moment to look around and understand the fundamentals of my success.

During the sudden and rather abrupt financial climate change I found myself in disbelief, how on earth could development and construction cease to exist? Within a very short window my world changed from thriving to surviving.

SURVIVAL MODE.....

So why did I walk to work? The moment my short term income quickly reduced to zero I made a very important decision to define wants and needs, so I didn't need to spend $125 per month for a parking space. This mentality continued through every aspect of my daily life, walking though the grocery store I would literally look at certain foods and question, "Do I really need this?" Turns out I managed to reduce my weekly grocery bill to less than $20, yet ate reasonably healthy. To save gas on the weekends, I rode my bike practically every place that wouldn't frown upon gym clothes drenched in sweat.

Looking back, I learned the true fundamentals of survival not necessarily in terms of fending off wolves with a campfire; it was mainly about finding the true foundation of daily living which will sustain not only health and happiness but also the rate at which cash burns. This is an incredibly important concept to understand when starting a business; profits are not realized until certain thresholds are met. A basic concept yes, but identifying the capital burn between return gaps will help measure the true mode of survival.

Survival doesn't require that you have to live in hindsight or pity the moment, it means understanding future requirements and effectively managing assets to not only outlive the period of survival, but to build a foundation that will sustain prosperity.

HURRICANE PRICES ARE PURE ECONOMICS....

October 23, 2005, living in Delray Beach Florida, the local news weather team and I seemed convinced that Hurricane Wilma would be a non-event for the East Coast of South Florida. With Wilma lingering just North of Key West, I checked into bed around 10 p.m. Roughly four hours later I suddenly woke to what sounded like a freight train outside my window. As I walked outside it seemed something was very wrong, my suspicions were verified when I watched a piece of roofing material dangle in the air then quickly track towards my direction. While I ran for cover I quickly turned to watch the debris smash into my window; as if that were not enough, the power went down shortly after.

I later discovered that Wilma took a quick easterly direction and absolutely pounded South Florida. Since we were not expecting such a destructive storm of course nobody was prepared, including myself. I had quarter of a tank of gas, two used batteries and a refrigerator of food that was quickly going bad. I drove to the local store to gather supplies and found a sea of people with the same idea, yet there seemed to be such anger in the air. The store was charging $20 per battery, $40 per buffet burner and nearly an arm or a leg for edible food. People were enraged and felt gouged; many purchased the bare essentials and went about their business. After gathering the minimal necessities myself, I noticed on my way out a man with several generators for sale at what seemed to be an astronomical price of $5,000, but was it? Driving home I noticed a gas station with at least 100 cars in line and a handmade sign which read "10 Gallon max for $100," a police officer was on the scene managing about a dozen angry buyers.

Many felt gouged and taken advantage of during a crisis. Several protested unfair pricing and purchase limits. The reality is this event exposed the true fundamentals of economics. As we all know, the law of supply and demand has a direct correlation to price. As demand rises or supply falls, then prices will rise.

Unfortunately hurricanes subject unusual changes to supply and demand which of course drive the value of essential goods to exponential levels. Let's dig deeper, drastic changes in demand can create a supply problem especially during events which interrupt the replenishment chain. Prior to Wilma's landfall, some decided to stock up on supplies. It was reported that many stores were extremely limited in survival materials. The problem here is, without price adjustment, these individuals purchased more than their needs required which lead to significant shortages.

To illustrate the impact of unexpected demand change without price adjustment, consider two scenarios:

A family of four is looking for batteries, flashlights and non-perishable food. When they arrive at the store it seems supplies are reasonably priced so naturally they purchase a flashlight for each member of the family, the required batteries and a stockpile for reserves. Also, they stock up with a food supply to last two weeks. Another family arrives at the store, batteries and flashlights are sold out and food is limited to perishable items.

Consider the same family seeking supplies, when they arrive at the store it appears prices are ten times the typical market value for all goods. This spike in cost requires the family to consider what they actually need. Are four flashlights and a massive stockpile of batteries needed? Is it necessary to buy two weeks' worth of food? Due to price increases, demand is managed to sustain supply to meet the needs of the next family.

The exponential increase in price of goods during a hurricane or any natural disaster may appear to be gouging the local population. However, rapid increase in price is a small price to pay for an adequate supply of essential goods.

EMOTION CREATES COMMOTION....

The sun goes up and the sun goes down every day, you can set your clock by it. Certain seasons the sun is further from or closer to earth, we know this through the study of cyclical patterns. Consider another cyclical pattern, if winter is coming then naturally prices or cold weather clothing rises and conversely prices drop during summer. The same is true for purchasing a car, certain time periods throughout the year automotive manufacturers provide fairly aggressive discounts to move inventory. Opportunity exists if you study patterns, understand the fundamentals and control emotional buying.

Let's review the fundamentals of the most recent Great Recession. Real Estate maintains sustainability by progressing through time at natural limits; low, mid and high. In the early 2000's, America experienced a rapid increase in intrinsic real estate value well above the natural high water mark of natural inflation. Like building Legos the perceived value of property rose at an increasing rate according to related comparable transactions. The problem is that perception turned into emotion. The moment I knew we were headed for trouble was during a conversation with a residential broker during a property tour in 2005. She said with a sense of urgency, "If you act quickly and your offer is high enough, buying this property will be the equivalent of buying a winning lottery ticket."

While the thought of buying a winning lottery ticket sounds wonderful, the fundamentals of price relative to value over decades of historical patterns pointed to one conclusion, we are headed for a brick wall. Now, this is the moment of opportunity. As Baron Rothschild once said, "Buy when there's blood in the streets." With real estate values set to take a steep decline, investors with adequate liquid capital seized the ability to capture assets at severely depressed prices.

If hindsight is 20/20 then learn, adapt and grow your ability to capitalize on upcoming trends. Jim Cramer once gave us an excellent opportunity indicator; he identified a correlation between stock trends and news. When a single news outlet is reporting on upward trends in value chances are it's a good buy. When three or more news stations are reporting on the same news the window of opportunity has likely closed. Here is a similar real estate example, when individuals with zero experience in residential or commercial investments suddenly become developers or "flippers" chances are the trend is at the end of its run.

As untrained individuals enter a complex field, common mistakes can be catastrophic. Consider an investment on a 20,000 square foot industrial building. In South Orlando this property would cost roughly $65.00 per square foot to produce. As a Net, Net, Net return, the base rent for this facility could range in the $4.50 – $5.00 per square foot range depending on function and location. Generally an acceptable capitalization rate would be 7%, considering low estimated rent the building value would be $1,285,714. If an untrained investor purchases the property for $2,000,000 the investment would never make sense because the natural base rate could not achieve equilibrium given the market parameters.

Emotional actions will not allow you to experience the true purpose of the decision. Just like the sun and seasonal patterns trends can be found in almost any aspect of life and business – if everyone else is making the same investment then position ahead of the cyclical top end and prepare for the shift.

As I started my career at the absolute bottom of the market I learned to make decisions based on fact not emotion. Surviving on rice and frozen chicken taught me the importance of identifying the most important elements of my business, and that acting on emotion clouds the ability to differentiate between wants and needs.

Study historical trends and stick to the fundamentals to eliminate the tendency to make emotional decisions. Anticipate changes in market conditions and look to adjust strategy to capitalize on foreseeable opportunities.

About Eric

Eric is a native Floridian raised in Tampa while being surrounded by the Development and Construction Industry through the family business. He is blessed with his loving wife Lindsay, their daughter Isla and two amazing pups, Marley and Cooper. Eric is a graduate of The University of North Florida, where he received a Bachelor of Science in Construction and Real Estate Development.

Currently, Eric is the Director of Leasing for the Orlando portfolio of DCT Industrial where he specializes in leasing, development and acquisition of industrial properties in the Central Florida commercial real estate market. Prior to joining DCT Industrial, Eric provided leasing services for over 4 million square feet of industrial real estate from 2009 to 2013. From 2001 to 2009 he developed and constructed over 3 million square feet of real estate and successfully negotiated over $500 million in project contracts. Eric was also recently featured in *Newsweek Magazine* as one of America's PremierExperts®.

As an innovative entrepreneur, Eric also owns and operates a seasonal Christmas tree business in Winter Park, Florida, whereby he has successfully built and maintained a brand that is well known for delivering a quality product with a focus on superior service.

If you would like more information about Eric Penaranda, or would like to discuss commercial real estate in any market, call him at: 407-222-2424.

CHAPTER 16

THE "WORRY FREE" REAL ESTATE TRANSACTION

BY DAVE BOWEN

I've always had a goal with every client that I've worked with, and that is to create a completely "worry free" transaction. I can't promise "trouble free," as there are things that extend beyond my control, but when I'm working with a client on their transaction, I've learned the strategies to make their very important process a smoother one. And it has made all the difference.

> *If you want a real professional handling your Real Estate needs, you want to hire Dave. If you want a smooth and with 'no surprises' experience all the way through to closing, you want to hire Dave. He did an amazing job and I would recommend him to anyone.*
> ~Zillow, Millerjl55

We can all agree that there is no shortage of Realtors, but there is a difference amongst the many out there when it comes to the level of service they offer and if they honor their word. Before entering into real estate, I worked in the automotive industry and consistent themes in that industry that carry over to the real estate industry include:

- Logic and reasoning
- Gaining rapport and trust through effective communication, thereby learning what the true questions and oppositions to a deal may be—it's often below the "surface"
- Being a person of your word

These things are important because they help to anticipate challenges ahead of time and prepare for them. Taking the best initiatives to eliminate surprises is a strategy that offers peace of mind to the client, which is an integral part of the Realtor/client relationship.

In order to be of the best service possible, I've put a focus on sellers in my career, finding a wonderful partner to put "worry free" focus on the buying side of transactions. It's lead to a process that is rooted in sound results and expertise that makes the difference in the sale of a home.

HOW I HELP GUIDE SELLERS THROUGH THE PROCESS OF SELLING THEIR HOME DETERMINES THE EXPERIENCE THEY HAVE

By investing energy in the entire process of working with someone to sell a home, I have to always be thinking ahead. This insight and proactive manner helps my clients to see me in action, knowing that I am indeed vested in their best interests and outcomes. Their kind words to me face-to-face, and the testimonies that they put on sites such as Zillow, are of great value to me and are the most rewarding part of my career.

Dave was a great Realtor to work with. Not only he was very knowledgeable and experienced in the local market, but he also was able to answer all our questions right away...
~Zillow, Redder

A common question that I'm often asked by friends and potential clients is how they can effectively determine who the best Realtor to work with is. I love this question, because I am an open book, wanting to share my knowledge and information. It helps me to better connect with my clients. Before we even meet face to face, I consider my role to be one of a helper, not just to be the showman that dazzles them until they sign on the dotted line.

From my perspective, these points are important to consider when choosing a Realtor:

FINDING A REALOR WHO "FITS" YOU

Not all Realtors are meant for all clients. You want one who will actually do what they say. To know which Realtor that is, consider these three qualities, as they should be easily and eagerly demonstrated by a quality Realtor:

- **Trustworthiness:** They can explain how they look out for your interests, and that their fiduciary responsibility is to you. Testimonials (particularly online) are a wonderful way to discover if any potential Realtor has a proven record of delivering what they say they will.
- **Confidence:** Does their knowledge and expertise show in how they talk with you? Before I go into an appointment to earn a listing for a property, it takes a lot of research and diligence. I want to know the neighborhood, the pertinent information, and be able to have a real conversation with any potential client the first time we meet.
- **Honesty:** Believe it or not, the best answer you can hear at times from a Realtor is, "No." It can be a great sign of integrity and show you that a good Realtor will not say or do anything to get the deal. You need to have realistic expectations of what will make your home move. That is how you can recognize that your chances of having a "worry free" transaction are important. Furthermore, a "no" with good reasons leaves an opportunity for knowledge and sound ideas to be presented, showing what is reasonable to expect and hope for.

ALLOW YOUR AGENT TO REPRESENT YOU AND YOUR INTERESTS

Real estate transactions can be long, and at times, difficult. You need to believe in your agent and their training and professional expertise, allowing them to represent you effectively, and with your goals in mind. This assurance comes with:

- **Experience:** The time that a Realtor has been in business and the volume of business they do does matter. And while everyone deserves a chance, you don't want to make an emotional decision and hire someone you're uncertain about, just to be nice. You have real concerns that require expertise.
- **Personality:** It is good to have a positive rapport with your Realtor. This often makes the difference between feeling stressed and anxious or confident that your transaction is a priority to them and it's getting the proper amount of attention.
- **Accessibility:** Determine what is an acceptable response time to you in regards to communication. What are acceptable waiting periods for returning telephone calls, responding to emails, and answering questions? If you feel that calls should be returned to you within six hours and you are considering someone who says twenty-four hours, that agent isn't as accessible for you as you require.

With the right Realtor chosen, it's time to think about everything that goes into a successful transaction. Because the more your chosen agent knows and shares with you, the better your experience will be.

From the time I signed the listing to after the house sold (which was only about 2 months) he followed through on every detail and was always available to answer my questions and guide me through the process.
~Zillow, Auction4u

KNOWLEDGE AND NUANCES OF THE DEAL

For me, a thorough understanding of the full gamut of real estate is a critical requirement of my profession. Yes, there are professionals in various areas, but it's my responsibility to be a wealth of knowledge for my clients, tapping into information when asked about it. This includes: types of construction, common defects, equipment, the overall process, general mortgage savvy, negotiations, and the ability to propose alternatives that work for all involved parties as the need arises.

Knowledge and initiative often makes the difference between a failed contract and happy sellers handing over keys to a buyer at the closing table.

Houses are real, predictable, and consistent. People, however, are more fluid and unpredictable, responding in different ways to the same situations and questions. The quality of dialogue between the Realtor and client is everything, because it can lead to resolving problems before they escalate.

There is a fair amount of time between the listing of a property to receiving a contract on it, and then eventually closing. This is where knowledge about the nuances of a deal really comes into play. Realtors need to understand the process and flow of:

- **Fair negotiations:** Negotiations need to be fair to both sides. Quick fixes, where one side takes advantage of the other's naiveté, usually unravel when the "victim" figures it out. Everyone deserves respect in a good real estate transaction.
- **Timing:** Avoiding emotionally-charged confrontations is professional and smart. The single biggest cause of "For Sale By Owner" negotiations and/or contract failures is someone being offended by what the other party said. Professionals make this difficult task appear simple, as they have experience and training guiding them.
- **Inspections:** If there are required repairs that were not

foreseen how are they addressed? Efficiently, so they don't create delays?

- **Appraisals:** Sound groundwork to determine a solid value in the beginning and only accepting deals that are "closable" are necessary for avoiding appraisal issues, such as coming in lower than the purchase price.
- **Loan approvals:** Different types of loans take different lengths of time and have different requirements; sharing insight into this with clients is important, because it's when we don't know or understand something that the unpredictability of the human response really shows itself. Don't hesitate to ask any agent you are considering working with about these things. I know that if someone were to ask me, I could answer questions confidently and accurately, because I do my homework in order to work best for my clients.

THE PREPARATION FOR THE LISTING

I pride myself in being able to determine what really is the obstacle with sellers and their properties. Preparing a home for sale has to be about more than just tossing money at solutions; it's also creative and that is part of the distinction that I offer.

Dave Bowen made selling our home an easy and wonderful experience. His knowledge and professionalism is unsurpassed. I would recommend him to anyone selling or buying a home.
~Zillow, smsebelle

Here are nine things to take into consideration when preparing to sell a property:

1. **Condition of the home:** Is it retail ready, or a wholesale property that an investor might purchase to fix-up and resell (flip)?

2. **Review the market:** A thorough market review offers

insight to answer these important and relevant questions:

- Are we in a buyer's or seller's market?
- What are the market conditions, recent sales, and current inventory?
- What are the list prices of comparable homes that are for sale? Most buyers will not overpay for a home.
- How long are most sales taking?
- Is it a market where sellers are contributing to the buyer's closing expenses? This is very common for first time home-buyers.

Knowing all of this matters, and Realtors do have access to the answers through the MLS. If they are not utilizing this invaluable resource, are they really a smart choice for you?

3. **Potential mechanical issues:** First, buyers will look at the cosmetic items to decide if they like the look and feel of a home, then it moves on to the mechanics. Faulty mechanicals can impede a sale. Professionals are familiar with the "4 Point Inspection" that is used by insurance companies, appraisers, and good listing agents. It includes:

   - Roofing
   - Plumbing
   - Electrical
   - HVAC

   Are these systems operating properly? Are they beyond their expected life? This should be disclosed and addressed right away. They will show up on an inspection, and a problematic inspection will likely bring re-negotiating for a lower price or certain seller concessions. Insurance companies have also been known to refuse coverage on homes with these mechanical issues. By acknowledging and addressing potential problems upfront you give yourself options. It may be prudent to remedy the situation before listing the home, as poor inspections often spook buyers enough that they will withdraw their offer, not giving the seller a chance to even work with them.

4. **Rotted wood and termite damage:** These are costly repairs and many government-backed loans (FHA and VA) require a clean Wood Destroying Organism (WDO) report. Taking care of any issues in regards to this upfront will help you to avoid difficulties that will arise in buyer financing (if it doesn't make them change their minds first).

5. **Roof condition:** The roof integrity is important to lenders and insurers, as it is an expensive repair if it leaks or fails. Inspectors will notice if a home needs a new roof as well. What happens most often when a bad roof is discovered? The seller has to agree to replace it or the buyer will cancel the contract. Addressing a new roof prior to the listing makes the most sense, as new roofs appeal to buyers and they will pay a premium for a home that has one.

6. **Presentation:** With over 80% of buyers searching houses on the internet now, you'll want to have a large number of high quality photographs to capture potential buyers' interest. You want to inspire them to come and view the house in person! To take good photos you will want to:

    - Make sure there is no clutter in the images. Photos like this can appear overwhelming and are just a click of-the-mouse away from someone taking a pass.
    - Stage the house, if necessary, to make it have "picture appeal."
    - Use a real camera, not a cellphone to take the pictures. Cell phone photos are for evidence, not marketing.

7. **Trim trees and shrubs:** When out of control, trees and shrubs make houses darker inside and can lead to pest infestations. Shrubs and vines should never reach the eaves, as they become "bug ladders" at that point. As a great

addition, some fresh annuals can make your house look more inviting.

8. **Door aesthetics:** Painting your front door and installing new lock hardware is a smart move, as this is what a potential buyer will see first. You want it to look impressive and inviting, not worn out. This is also a relatively inexpensive improvement.

9. **Touch up interior and exterior paint:** Warm, inviting, and neutral colors work best. Otherwise, buyers will already think of the work they need to do "right away" if they were to buy the house. It may seem dull, but the "Boring Builder Beige" color is your friend as a seller. Nobody loves it, but nobody hates it either.

It's important for sellers to acknowledge that the very personal experience of buying a home is about more than just money and price. Yes, money matters, but it is not the final deciding factor. As a seller, the more you can prepare your home for a better sale by following some guidance and proven experiences from your Realtor, the closer you will come to the "worry free" transaction.

IT'S THE INTANGIBLES THAT CREATE DISTINCTION

The level of comfort that I offer clients guides them throughout their entire real estate process, and it is what will stick with them long after the keys have been handed over. In the end, people will always remember how their transaction made them feel.

Closing day is much more than a relief,
it is a celebration of a new beginning.

About Dave

Dave Bowen's career in real estate started just after the "boom" that ended in 2005. He has over two decades of experience in customer service and management in the automobile sales and repair industry. These positions enabled him to develop the skills to listen to what his clients and the other side is asking for, and use that information, combined with his knowledge, to build an agreement that culminates in success for his client and referrals from them down the road.

Dave prides himself on spending sufficient time with each of his clients to fully understand their needs and to ensure their questions are all answered in a complete and truthful manner.

Dave is proud to be married, for more than three decades, to his high school sweetheart and equally proud of their son who is attending Florida State University.

If you are looking for a professional, knowledgeable and experienced agent who will not only help you to buy or sell a home, but also navigate you through the many potential snags along the way, Dave would look forward to working with you.

Contact info:

- Call or Text: 407-733-5755
- Email: DaveBowen@realtor.com
- www.BowenRealtors.com

CHAPTER 17

THE ART OF THE DEAL:
NEGOTIATIONS

BY JW DICKS, ESQ.

Real estate mogul Donald Trump called negotiating "the art of the deal" and used that phrase as the title of his first book. Country music legend Kenny Rogers sang, "You've got to know when to hold 'em, and know when to fold 'em." They were both right. Negotiating is an art that has to be learned. And one of the key elements is knowing when to hold onto your position and when to wait for a better deal. Between those two extremes a lot of money is made and lost. It's true that to a certain extent negotiators are born, not made. To some degree at least, the ability to hammer out a good deal is a God-given talent that some people are blessed with and some aren't—just as a few of us are blessed with a 95-mile-an-hour fastball, and most of us aren't. But that doesn't mean you can't improve on what you have and get better than you are, no matter what your level is at this moment. Even the greatest pitchers have a pitching coach, and Donald Trump learned about real estate deals at his father's knee. So education and training can help you get better at whatever you do, including negotiation.

This chapter focuses on skills taught to me by my mentors. We're also going to discuss some lessons taught to me in the School of

Hard Knocks, when someone more skilled than I was "ate my lunch" at the table. Hey, it happens to the best of us. Sometimes, if the other side is very good at what it does, you don't even know it has happened. And sometimes, you're happy that you learned something new, even if it was at your own expense.

NEGOTIATION STRATEGY #1: UNDERSTAND THAT "NO" DOESN'T ALWAYS MEAN "NO"

If you want a great lesson in negotiating, spend a day with a 5-year-old. They're the best. First, they're fearless, because they're too young to have been burned very often. Second, they're very much into themselves, because neither their parents nor their teachers have been able to break them of the habit of being what they want to be or getting what they want to get.

If a 5-year-old wants a piece of candy, he isn't going to ask you just one time and take your first "no" as the final answer. No, indeed! He'll ask you until you say "yes," or at least make a counteroffer that sounds acceptable.

This is the first rule of negotiating. "No" is just the beginning. "No" is the first step in finding out exactly what the other side means and how that position can be viewed in a positive light. You might as well face it from the beginning: Negotiating is the process of getting rejected. In fact, it's the very process of rejection, bad as it sometimes feels, that gives you the opportunity to find out what the other side really means. If you hate rejection, get over it or find someone else who handles it better and can be the negotiator in your stead.

This isn't necessarily an admission of failure. Many times, I used third parties to handle negotiations because they can often say and do things that you can't do for yourself.

Additionally, if you use another person as a middleman negotiator, that person can always bow out if things don't go well, and you can ride in on your white horse and save the day for both sides. The point is that you need to understand the process, recognize your skills or lack thereof, and create an environment of negotiating that works for you—no matter who's actually running the process.

NEGOTIATION STRATEGY #2: CONTROL THE PLAYING FIELD

In football, as in most sports, there's something called the "home field advantage." In fact, much of the football season is played with one eye on getting into a position where your team will have the home field advantage in the playoffs.

The playing field in real estate is equally important. You want to control the context, and the process, as much as you can. One of the most skilled negotiators we know is an attorney whom we've dealt with on many occasions. Sometimes he's on our side of the transaction, and (unfortunately) sometimes he's on the other side, representing himself or one of his companies. When he negotiates, he always tries to control the playing field by being the first to introduce the contract to be used in the transaction. He isn't overly aggressive about it. On the contrary, he's pointedly helpful, always offering to manage the process of creating the contract document.

Very few people turn down his offer. Why? Because it's expensive for them to hire an attorney, because drafting contracts is time-consuming, and because in some of the complicated transactions he's involved in, it's very difficult to structure contracts both creatively and in a legally enforceable way. So most people readily relinquish that responsibility. When they do, they give up a lot. While the contract isn't the only element of control in a real estate transaction, it's an important one. Frequently, it defines the terms of the deal, and if you're the one who originally defines what things mean, then you start with a big advantage.

The first thing you need to find out is what type of contract you're dealing with. If it's a so-called "standard contract," you immediately need ask, What kind of "standard"? Is it a standard buyer's contract, a standard seller's contract, or something else entirely? The distinction is important because there's a big difference. Here's one example from a contract that favors the seller: The buyer shall be given 15 days to inspect the property. But suppose the inspection clause reads as follows: The buyer shall be given 60 days to conduct a property inspection by an inspector of his choice. In the event the buyer determines that the property fails the inspection, at his sole discretion, then buyer and seller shall have 90 days to correct any deficiency.

Well, it still looks reasonably fair. After all, 60 days doesn't seem like too much time to arrange for an inspection, especially in a busy market. But the buyer actually has 150 days (i.e., 60 + 90) just for the inspection process. The drafter of the contract has in effect created a five-month option on the property for the buyer, where he can control what happens to the property without having any money at risk. In today's real estate environment, five months is an eternity. You can control the propertythe new rise in real estate and, ultimately, keep it, flip it or walk away. This flexibility is gained just by setting the table to your advantage.

Some of you may be thinking, "I would never sign a contract like that!" And maybe you wouldn't. But the reality is it happens all the time. First, in most cases, the "60 + 90" issue (or the equivalent) never even gets red-flagged in discussions.

Most people, even lawyers, read contracts very quickly, and a simple, boring clause like this tends to get lost in a multipage legal document. Second, the inspection clause doesn't sound particularly one-sided because the language says, "The buyer and the seller are given this time?" Hey, that's fair, isn't it? Not really, but it sounds fair enough.

Even if the party objects to "60 days"; they'll probably demand only that it be reduced from 60 to 30 days. If my attorney friend was in the deal and the issue was raised, he'd quickly volunteer to change it to 30 days, adding something like, "No problem at all; it's just the inspection we're talking about here?" In the process, he'd make you (the seller) feel slightly foolish for even raising the issue. And henceforth, you'd feel that much more uncomfortable about raising other issues in the contract, including far more important ones.

Here are several other ways to control the playing field in a real estate transaction:

1. ***Meet your counterpart in your office.*** In your office, you control the environment and the administrative staff. But as with all rules, you'll find there are times to make exceptions.

   Sometimes you may want to meet in the other party's office so he's more comfortable. It depends on the situation. It's part of the art of negotiating.

2. ***Control the production of any documents in your transactions.*** This includes contracts and leases. As I've already said, controlling the workflow controls what the document says at the outset. Of course, it's likely to get changed as the negotiations go back and forth, but at least the contract and other document start out the way you want them to. Following this rule will cost you out-of-pocket money, because in most cases it means your attorney will be doing the drafting, and you'll be paying the bill.

   But concentrating on these relatively small amounts of money is a huge mistake, especially if it means giving up control of the contract process.

3. ***Control the closing.*** All other things being equal, you want to hire the closing agent and name the place of closing. This isn't to imply that either you or the closing agent will do

anything underhanded. What you're trying to do is control the environment, making it easy to move a transaction along. If people are stressed because of their environment, they're more likely to be argumentative, even on small points.

A closing by its very nature is adversarial. By custom, the parties meet in the same room, each hears the financial picture from the other side, and anything one party dislikes necessitates a shift of money from one side of the table to the other. I don't like these types of closings. I often try to arrange separate times for the buyer and seller to sign documents—or, at a minimum, arrange separate rooms. Yes, this sometimes results in delays, when the other party has a problem that needs my input. To counter this, I tell the closing agent how to get in touch with me if needed.

4. ***Control who inspects the property.*** If you hire the inspector, you know she's going to be looking after your interests. When possible, I always try to be present when any inspections are done so I can hear the informal comments about the inspection. Sometimes the inspector will know the property, or at least the area, and by talking about it will give you extremely valuable information.

5. ***Control who conducts the property survey.*** The survey shows you encroachments on the property. If you're writing the check and talking to the surveyor directly, you'll find out more than if you don't speak to him. Encroachments, even small ones, can be a thorny problem, because they most often involve your direct neighbor. Commonsense tells you that you don't want to start off on a bad footing with your neighbors if you don't have to. If there's an encroachment, have the seller clean it up before closing, because she'll be moving. Let her be the bad guy.

6. ***Control who writes the title policy, particularly the exceptions in the policy.*** I've already addressed this

challenge. Title exceptions are what the title company says it isn't covering. If you don't read these exceptions and get the company to delete them from the policy, you aren't buying much coverage. Title companies have been at this a long time, and their data centers know what to exclude. Don't let them do it.

7. ***Control which lender is used and which financing terms are acceptable.*** The buyer chooses the lender, of course, but the seller can affect the terms by eliminating language favorable to the buyer in the contract. For example, if the contract says, "subject to the buyer getting financing at the prevailing rate," you as the buyer are much more locked into the deal than if the contract says, "subject to the buyer getting financing on terms acceptable to him at his sole discretion."

8. ***Control the type of deed to be issued.*** A "general warranty" deed conveys the most rights, so as a buyer that's what you always want the seller to give you. A "quit claim" deed conveys the fewest rights; for example, it doesn't even warrant that the seller owns the property. Make sure you're getting the type of deed you want and need.

NEGOTIATION STRATEGY #3: USE A PARTNER TO HEAD OFF PRESSURE RESPONSES

Let's imagine you're sitting at the table facing the other party in a real estate transaction, and a serious problem pops up. What next? If you're the decision maker on your side, you may feel compelled to make a decision right there on the spot. If you're an old hand in the industry and are experienced at negotiations, you may do fine under this kind of pressure. But the less experienced you are, the more it can cost you, because you aren't conversant with all the moving parts of a transaction. If you're up against a skilled player, she'll know exactly how to put you into a position of making a decision at exactly the most inopportune time for you.

Successful real estate players like Donald Trump conduct their negotiations themselves. Why? Because they've been in business so long that they know where they can go with a particular transaction, and they can think on the spot. (They also recognize that their presence alone may have a positive influence on the negotiation.) If you don't have this kind of experience and stature, your best course of action may be to say, "Let me check with my partner."

It doesn't matter what kind of partner you're referring to. Maybe it's a business partner, or your spouse, or just an associate whose advice you value. The point is, you need to buy a little extra time to think about what was just offered or rejected, and maybe get that partner's advice.

You can also use this strategy to turn the tables in your favor. For example, you could say, "Well, that seems reasonable enough, but I really need to discuss it with my partner. So let's go ahead and put it in writing, and I'll take it to him to discuss."

See how you've changed the playing field? You've required the other side to put its position in writing, and you've bought yourself a period of time to think about this new position—without the other side being able to change its mind easily. If you're a buyer, this move is almost always to your advantage because you can effectively take the property off the market for at least that period of time.

NEGOTIATION STRATEGY #4: USE THE POWER OF SILENCE

"You can hear a lot by listening," as the legendary Yogi Berra is supposed to have said.

This quote reminds us that listening is one of the most important aspects of negotiating. Normally, the more you talk, the more you lose, because you give the other side more and more information about your true bargaining stance, and that rarely helps you get the best deal.

There are some very bright people on my staff whom I never take to a negotiation, because there's no telling what they'll say. Their disclosures are innocent and well intentioned, but they tend to hurt our negotiating position. Think about it.

Assume you're buying a property. What signal does your team send when one of its members says, "Oh, we have the perfect furniture for this room!"? It tells the other side, loud and clear, that you've already mentally bought the property and moved in. As soon as this has been said, you can forget about negotiating, because the seller knows you'll back down.

Sellers also often give away the store by giving little hints about what's happening in their lives—if you can get them talking. I was once negotiating to buy a house. In talking to the wife of the couple who owned the property, she happened to mention that she was going away that weekend. When I asked where, she said she was flying up to see her husband, who had already moved on to his new job. Then and there, I knew that the sellers were likely to be very flexible in their negotiations because I knew the couple was now living apart. The point is, always be cautious about what you're saying and mindful about the information you may be giving to the other side.

When in negotiations, try thinking of yourself as a counselor. Your job is to be open and to ask questions in a warm and friendly matter. Act as if you're going to try to help the other side with its problem, because, in fact, you are. Listen to the other side's comments, and ask friendly follow-up questions. The more you can learn, the more likely it is that you can formulate an offer that will work both for you and for them. Approaching negotiations in this vein is more fun, often more successful, and personally more rewarding. And if you meet this same party in another transaction, that deal may prove even more successful.

NEGOTIATION STRATEGY #5: EMPLOY TAKE-AWAY OPTIONS

The most successful strategy I use, in almost all types of negotiations, is the "take-away." Frankly, I debated about whether to include it in this book because it works so well, and there's a chance that some of our opponents will read these pages. Ultimately, I decided that I couldn't leave out such a powerful strategy.

The take-away is used when a negotiation has reached a stalemate, or the other side is being unreasonable. When the other side says something like, "I wouldn't even consider that offer," your first response should be, "I understand exactly how you must feel." (This is a softening statement that sets up what's to follow.) You should then continue by saying something like, "We appreciate your time, and we hope we can work together sometime in the future," or some other appropriate sort of comment.

At that point, you can wait for the other side to respond, or you can just begin to pack up to leave. Whatever you do, keep quiet—because the next person who speaks…loses!

What you normally hear, after the silence, is a retraction of some or all of what the person just said. If you don't hear such a retraction, you'll know that the speaker was serious about his (unacceptable) position, and you might as well move on. Either way, you have the information you need: either to resume negotiations or to go to the next deal. You can't win them all, and time is money. The sooner you find out whether or not you're in the game, the better.

NEGOTIATION STRATEGY #6: USE THE "COLUMBO CLOSE"

You may recall the television series "Columbo," in which Peter Falk played the role of a detective who appeared to be a bumbler.

In fact, the bumbling was a tactic. When interviewing a suspect, he'd ask lots of questions, then, when he was finished, he'd get up to leave. But when he was almost out the door, he'd turn and say, "Ah, just one more question." That question would always turn out to be the zinger. The suspect, thinking the grilling was over, would be caught off guard. The tables were turned. In negotiations, the "Columbo close" can be used in a similar fashion. Imagine you're in the final phase of your negotiation. Everything seems to be done. Then, in your best Peter Falk voice, you casually ask, "You know, I was just wondering if . . ."

You'll have to fill in the rest of the sentence. Maybe it's, "You know, I was just thinking, if you don't mind, could we make the inspection period 90 days, instead of 30? I really would be more comfortable, if that's OK with you."

Or maybe, "You know, if we increased the price I pay you for the property, but you agreed to pay all the closing costs, it would save me having to pay cash out of my pocket, and you'd get the same net cash from the sale. That works for you, doesn't it? And you'll be amazed at how often it will work for them.

NEGOTIATION STRATEGY #7: USE A CONVERSATIONAL APPROACH

Everyone ultimately develops his or her own style of negotiating. Some people are reserved, some are loud, and others fall somewhere between the two extremes. It really doesn't matter which style you use; you just have to determine what works best for you. One style that works for many people is a conversational approach, centered on questions that are used to determine the seller's objectives in relation to price, terms and timing—the three factors that will determine the deal. I've found that questions starting with "would you" or "could you" work best because they convey consideration and thoughtfulness.

For example, if the seller says he wants 20 percent down, and that amount doesn't work for you, your response could be, "Well, would you consider breaking that up for me, with 10 percent down and a note for the balance in two years at 8 percent? Or "Could you break that up for me, and take 10 percent now and the balance in a note at 8 percent?" If you ask the question in a nonthreatening manner, it's likely to be received that way by the other party. He may still say "no," but if he does, he'll often say why, and that answer will give you more information as to what he's trying to accomplish.

The more you can find out about what the other side needs, the better you can structure the deal to meet those objectives, instead of simply getting into an unproductive cycle of offer and counteroffer. You may ultimately find that there's no good deal available for you. Well, again, the faster you find that out, the faster you can move on to something else.

NEGOTIATION STRATEGY #8: USE YOUR STAR NEGOTIATOR

There's a common assumption among many authors of real estate books that you should handle your own negotiations. I don't agree. The person who should negotiate your deal is the one who's most likely to bring about a success. Sometimes that's you, and sometimes it isn't.

Earlier, I pointed out that great negotiators (like great athletes) have a gift. You want the best person on your team—your star negotiator— making your arguments for you. If that's you, great. If it isn't, then find the best person in your network of professionals to do it for you.

After years of experience in many different circumstances, I consider myself to be a very good negotiator. But I'm well aware that there are many situations where there are better people for the job. Sometimes I use people who have a relationship with the other side of the transaction. Sometimes a development deal

I'm doing requires a credible expert— on, say, environmental problems—to explain my stance on that issue to the other side. The point is, if for any reason you feel that someone else can negotiate better than you, be humble and wise enough to admit it and bring that person in. Your goal is to bring about a successful deal, and that may mean that you do nothing but find the deals and turn them over to someone with the skills to represent you in the rest of the transaction. Don't lose focus on your deal-making objective.

NEGOTIATION STRATEGY #9: NEVER NEGOTIATE AGAINST YOURSELF

One serious mistake in negotiation is to make decisions on behalf of the other party. For example, suppose you're preparing to make an offer that you think is realistic. But then you think, "Uh oh, the seller isn't going to accept that!" Then you raise your offer even before the seller hears it. Before you say that you would never do something that foolish, let us assert that everybody does it, and often for an honorable reason: We tend to put ourselves in the other person's shoes. Well, try not to do that if it leads you to negotiate against yourself. Structure your offer based on what works for you, and let the seller make up her own mind. You may be pleasantly surprised.

Another time this comes up is when you make an offer, and the seller doesn't do anything in response, so you make another offer. Don't bid against yourself! Get the other party to counter, even if it's for full price. At least if you get a full-price counter, you can bind the contract with just your signature. Remember, time is money. If the other party doesn't counter and you make yet another offer, you're wasting a lot of time.

NEGOTIATION STRATEGY #10: DON'T FALL IN LOVE WITH THE DEAL

If you fall in love with the deal, it's going to cost you. The motto for negotiations is, and always will be, he who cares less, wins.

There are many reasons to fall in love with a deal. Sometimes we fall in love with the property. (I've warned you about that!) Sometimes we get wrapped up in a deal because we've told people we were doing it. Sometimes we fall in love with a deal because we've already spent the profits, at least in our mind's eye.

Don't fall victim to these kinds of mistakes. The best deals you make are the ones that you have carefully analyzed and structured to meet your needs. If you depart from the script because you "want to do the deal," you're almost sure to make mistakes. I've done this myself, and it has been expensive.

Negotiating is an art. It requires a solid knowledge of your product and your goals, and the ability to think on your feet. Some of you will be very good at this. All of you can get better; it just takes practice. And it helps a great deal if you can learn to enjoy the process as you go.

THE NEGOTIATIONS CHECKLIST

- ***Don't take rejection personally.*** Learn to deal with the word no. It's nothing personal. The word "no" is often followed by the word "because," and the words that follow "because" often tell you what you need to know in order to succeed.

- ***Do what you can to control the playing field.*** The home-field advantage is real. You want to control both the context and the process, if possible. One way to do this is to take on (or have your lawyer take on) tasks that are either burdensome or complex. The person who controls the text of the evolving agreement, for example, holds a lot of power.

- ***Don't get stampeded.*** If you start feeling pressured—say, in response to a new offer that has just been put on the table—resist that pressure. Say that you'd like that last offer in writing so your partner can review it. It doesn't much matter who your partner is, or even if you have one. You need to buy time and (most likely) get some outside advice about this new offer.

- ***Listen more than you talk.*** People love to talk about themselves. Use that fact to your advantage—and meanwhile, refrain from talking too much yourself.

- ***Use take-aways, the Colombo close, and would-you's.*** Every negotiation is different. Each has its own rhythm and takes its own twists and turns. Get familiar with a range of negotiating tactics, and use them when they're helpful. The goal with all such tactics should be to either: 1) close the deal, or 2) find out that there's no deal to be had.

- ***Never negotiate against yourself.*** It sounds too obvious to dwell on, but everybody does it. Put your best offer together, and give the other side a chance to respond. Don't second-guess yourself before the other party has even had a chance to respond. (Again, you'll be wasting your valuable time.)

- ***Never, never fall in love with the deal.*** It's the same idea as "never falling in love with a building." Don't let a deal get its own momentum. It doesn't matter if you've got an ego stake in making it work. If it can't work, let it go. The deals you fall in love with tend to get very expensive.

About JW

JW Dicks, Esq., is a Wall Street Journal Best-Selling Author®, Emmy Award-Winning Producer, publisher, board member, and co-founder of organizations such as The National Academy of Best-Selling Authors®, and The National Association of Experts, Writers and Speakers®.

JW is the CEO of DNAgency and is a strategic business development consultant to both domestic and international clients. He has been quoted on business and financial topics in national media such as *USA Today, The Wall Street Journal, Newsweek, Forbes, CNBC.com,* and *Fortune Magazine Small Business.*

Considered a thought leader and curator of information, JW has more than forty-three published business and legal books to his credit and has co-authored with legends like Jack Canfield, Brian Tracy, Tom Hopkins, Dr. Nido Qubein, Dr. Ivan Misner, Dan Kennedy, and Mari Smith. He is the Editor and Publisher of *ThoughtLeader® Magazine.*

JW is called the "Expert to the Experts" and has appeared on business television shows airing on ABC, NBC, CBS, and FOX affiliates around the country and co-produces and syndicates a line of franchised business television show such as *Success Today, Wall Street Today, Hollywood Live,* and *Profiles of Success.* He has received an Emmy® Award as Executive Producer of the film, *Mi Casa Hogar.*

JW and his wife of forty-three years, Linda, have two daughters, three granddaughters, and two Yorkies. He is a sixth-generation Floridian and splits his time between his home in Orlando and his beach house on Florida's west coast.